CHALLENGES AND PLEASURES

Living Ethically in a Competitive World

BARBARA CUTNEY

University Press of America, Inc.
Lanham • New York • Oxford

Copyright © 1997 by
University Press of America,® Inc.
4720 Boston Way
Lanham, Maryland 20706

12 Hid's Copse Rd.
Cummor Hill, Oxford OX2 9JJ

British Library Cataloging in Publication Information Available

Library of Congress Cataloging-in-Publication Data

Cutney, Barbara.
Challenges and pleasures : living ethically in a competitive world /
Barbara Cutney.
p.   cm.
1. Ethics. 2. Values. I. Title.
BJ1012.C88   1997   170--dc21   97-30567 CIP

ISBN 0-7618-0910-4 (pbk: alk. ppr.)

⊖™ The paper used in this publication meets the minimum
requirements of American National Standard for information
Sciences—Permanence of Paper for Printed Library Materials,
ANSI Z39.48—1984

—For Justine—

to celebrate courage, kindness, and compassion

Contents

PART TWO — LIVING MORALLY: DIFFICULTIES AND DETERRENTS

PART THREE — ETHICS: A "YES" TO LIFE

Foreword

I wrote this book in response to two specific concerns: one regarding the quality of people's lives; and the other regarding the prevalent confusion with respect to ethics and values.

The first of these was prompted by an awareness of people who experience a chronic sense of discontent and dissatisfaction. The reason for this state of mind, however, was not immediately apparent. Nor was it clear whether this troublesome condition could be avoided.

The second situation which led me to undertake this project is very different from the first. It is that I've heard people repeatedly refer to "values" and "ethics" in numerous dissimilar ways, some of which were clearly misleading. Bantering the terms "values" and "ethics" around in this inconsistent fashion could compound confusion about their meaning and significance.

After awhile it became obvious that these two seemingly disparate dimensions—our quality of life and our understanding of ethical living—were, in fact, related.

My task then came into focus. It was to demonstrate how the two are inextricably bound. To do this, I've set about explaining the nature of values and ethics and highlighting their importance. With this exposition as the foundation, I've made some suggestions for ways that we might live with greater satisfaction. For moral living can not only alleviate a number of distresses but also be a source of pleasure.

The ensuing discussion is grounded in commonly found experiences to show the impact ethics and values can have on everyday situations. The relationships between living morally and other issues of general concern—such as stress, loneliness, health, addiction and violence—are explored. Ideas about ethics, values, and the good life developed primarily by philosophers serve as the framework for this book and as the inspiration for many of its views. With this manuscript we continue in their footsteps, seeking a better understanding of how to live a good life.

I have made no attempt, however, to offer an account of the literature from which many of the concepts considered here have been derived, nor to replicate the subtlety of these scholarly works. Their full value can be appreciated only if the texts themselves are read. So I've included explanatory notes that refer the reader to several sources which amplify the ideas found in this book. These notes also offer additional explanations of why some issues have been raised.

At this point I want to thank every one of my friends—especially Gail August, Linda Millet, Andy Scott, and Anita Randolfi—for believing in this enterprise and supporting its development. Henry Perkinson, Richard Rumana, and Irene Mahoney made critical suggestions for the text's articulation in its early stages; for this I am grateful. Special appreciation is extended to Joseph Martos, Tom Colwell, and Justine Cutney Freitas for their generosity and encouragement every step of the way. I am also very thankful for the opportunity to work with Barbara Eubanks in the book's preparation; her respect for the text and her editorial expertise were invaluable.

Finally, I want to express appreciation to the University Seminars at Columbia University for assistance in the preparation of the manuscript for publication. Material drawn from this work was presented to the University Seminar on Moral Education.

Preface

Professor Barbara Cutney's *Challenges and Pleasures: Living Ethically in a Competitive World* is a breath of fresh air to students and educators alike who have had so many often exhausting and even fruitless encounters with the literature of moral philosophy and moral education— a literature which is above all intent on instructing us in the standard theories, problems, arguments, and recognized thinkers thought to be necessary to knowing what moral education is all about. In reading Professor Cutney's book, one is relieved to find these details pleasantly in the background. In their place, we are led through an extended series of thought-provoking questions which revolve around the experiences of ordinary people struggling to live ethically amid the complexities of the modern world.

Professor Cutney makes it clear that the ethical life is not easily realized in the competitive setting of modernity that challenges the traditional virtues and values which have emerged throughout the Western tradition and which still largely define the values we take to be moral. The materialism, commercialism, and relativism which play upon our sensibilities often make it difficult for us to see how these values might still guide us. Torn by ambivalence and indifference, we become "followers" or "drifters," bent upon "keeping up appearances," or worse, resorting to immoral behavior.

Professor Cutney vividly portrays the dilemma of morality in our time through numerous examples from her own life and the lives of friends and students. Yet she is confident that the ethical life can triumph. We are not pawns of our environment; we *can choose* to be ethical. She echoes Aristotle's "We become good by doing what the good man does" in saying we learn values by living with those who embrace them. "But whose values?" the skeptic might retort. Professor Cutney's answer to this strikes both a traditional and, if I am not mistaken, a postmodern note.

It is clear that she defines the moral and ethical in terms of the dominant values of the Western tradition. The Greek virtues, the values of Christianity, and the authority of reason are what consitute the substance of morality. But underlying these is an even more important element: the power of the moral self.

The inner moral self is the motor, we might say, of the ethical life. Informed by knowledge, it is capable of feelings of intense caring, conviction, and courage which give rise to moral action, to considerations of our own needs and aspirations and those of others.

Why, though, should the moral self exercise itself in this way? "Why should we be moral?" Though she does not quite put it this way, I believe Professor Cutney's answer is that it is part of human nature to do so, to resist and respond to adversity by asserting our concern for the universal human family.

It is in founding morality in the self that I see Professor Cutney touching at least one aspect of postmodern thought. Zygmunt Bauman, following in the footsteps of Emmanuel Lévinas, also claims that the self is the foundation of morality. As he puts it, the moral self is even "before being"—it has a sort of pre-ontological status.

> Taking responsibility for the other as if I were already responsible is an act of creation of the moral space...This responsibility which is taken 'as if it was already there' is the only foundation morality can have.[1]

Yet both Bauman and Lévinas recognize that this "pre-existing" self may be overcome by the social self.

> Conscience of the moral self is Humanity's only warrant and hope.[2] Fortunately for humanity...the moral conscience has only been anaesthetized, not amputated. It is still there, dormant perhaps, often stunned, sometimes shamed into silence, but capable of being awoken...[3]

---

1 Z. Baumann (1994), *Postmodern Ethics* (Cambridge, MA: Blackwell Pubs.), p. 75.
2 Ibid., p. 249.
3 Ibid.

Everything depends, then, on the "awakening" (or "sobering up") of the moral conscience—though for Bauman awakening is the two-way street:

> If one can awake or sober up, one can as well fall asleep and get inebriated. Uncertainty rocks the cradle of morality, fragility haunts it through life. There is nothing necessary in being moral. Being moral is a chance which must be taken up; yet it may also be, and as easily, forfeited.[4]

Professor Cutney would doubtless agree with Bauman. But her book offers moving testimony that the opportunity of morality is greater than its loss; that the possibility of awakening to it is more accessible than those disillusioned (or intoxicated) with the modern project can realize. *Challenges and Pleasures* is therefore a book about moral awakening, a task to which its nontechnical simplicity will offer a measure of success where many a dreary text has failed.

Tom Colwell
Professor of Philosophy of Education
Co-Director, M.A. Program in Environmental Conservation Education
New York University

---

4   Ibid., pp. 76-77.

Introduction

Look at the news—it abounds with stories of people who've been unethical:

EXECUTIVE EMBEZZLES CORPORATE FUNDS

YOUTH GANGS DEFACE NATIONAL MONUMENT

MOTHER ABANDONS NEWBORN INFANT

Critics assail modern society, proclaiming it's in more trouble than ever. Numerous books explore ethical issues and expose the unethical practices now occurring in business, medicine, and education.

World news reveals other cultures and their accepted practices. Oftentimes these customs are new to us and leave us feeling uncomfortable. For these ways of life are frequently discussed without a hint of how to evaluate them. We're left to our own devices. If, in response, we reject behavior foreign to us, we may begin to wonder whether we're just being narrow-minded. On the other hand, if we accept it, we may then question our own way of doing things.

Over the years the questions my college students have raised with respect to morality have radically changed. In the past they were concerned with how to make the best moral choices, inquiring about specific ethical issues. Today the questions students ask me have focused more and more on the value of the moral enterprise itself: "Why should I be ethical? Is there any good reason for being moral?" The students are perplexed. Having no satisfactory answers to these questions, they really don't know how they want to live. So they cannot get a handle on themselves and their lives.

Moreover, many adults are not content with their lives. They have been gravitating in large numbers to workshops, seminars and retreats in search of their inner child, their feelings, or their spiritual and higher self.

Something is missing. Something is awry.

What is it?

Why has it occurred?

Are these efforts to restore vibrancy and meaning to life related at all to living ethically?

Are there any compelling reasons for being moral?

These are key questions for us, as they have been for Socrates, Plato and other great thinkers. More than ever, these issues need to be re-addressed by us all. And that's just what this book is about.

To paint a broad picture, we'll start by looking at the dynamics of both ethical and unethical behavior. Then we'll explore the effects of each on ourselves, on others, and on our world.

My concern here is to help you better understand the nature of ethical and unethical life. To do this, I shall talk about moral action from different perspectives. (The words "ethical" and "moral" will be used interchangably throughout. The same goes for "unethical" and "immoral.")[1]

Sometimes we'll explore the inner dynamics of individuals, reflecting on the quality of moral life and the effects such a life can have on us and on others. At other times we'll examine patterns of behavior across a broad spectrum of society. This perspective will permit us to consider the ramifications of moral living on society at large. And lastly, while standing outside all specific contexts, we'll look at some salient features of a moral life.

So you see, our discussions will move back and forth between individual events and actions, societal patterns, and general ideas. For each of these elements contributes to our understanding of the others. By taking all of them into account, we are more likely to gain a better grasp of each one.

As you read, you may want to pursue the issues that are of interest to you. The notes at the end of the text suggest how you can begin.

But this book does more than present information for your understanding: it also provides a basis for re-evaluating your own choices, goals and values. And it suggests ways in which all of us can live more satisfying lives in today's world.

You see, the focus of my attention throughout is how we live: our choices and our actions. Now please don't get me wrong—I am deeply concerned about having laws and institutions that can promote moral life. But these structures will support ethical living *only* if they are created to do so and if the people who live with them use them for this end. Moral people are more likely than others to establish institutions and laws that are reflective of ethical ideals, and then to make sure that these goals are realized. The power to shape a moral society resides within us all. When each of us lives morally, the world becomes a more ethical place in which to live.

Before we proceed, let's be clear. This is not a "how-to" book. It will not tell you what to do or how to do it. Instead, it endeavors to broaden your understanding of values and ethics. This, in turn, can help you make more sense out of your life; and it may influence your decisions. So we will begin with how values and ethical actions affect our lives. Then we will continue by looking at how we can live ethically in today's world and why this can be considered worthwhile.

Please note: because this work raises many ideas for consideration, it is well-suited for reading in small segments.

The issues raised in the concluding chapters may very well tempt you to skip to the end of the book. But I assure you that the last chapters will make much more sense after you have read the earlier ones. Then you will be in a better position to appreciate my point that living ethically can be beneficial to you, to others, and to our world.

PART ONE

VALUES: THEY MAKE
A DIFFERENCE

Chapter I

ℰℭ

Values

A Foundation for Us

Values are embedded in human lives. Ethical action can be one of ours. So let's ask ourselves: Should we affirm moral behavior as a value?

To answer this, we'll first look at several roles values play in our lives.

Our values are reflected in the assessments we make. When we view something as a value, we may think of it as good, important, interesting, beautiful, obligatory; or as insignificant, tawdry, horrible, ugly, and so forth.

We care about the actions we assess positively and feel committed to them. Thus we find ourselves trying to do whatever is good and important to us. On the other hand, we respond negatively toward whatever we believe has little worth, and we may try to remove it from our lives.

It is often easier to understand people who share our values. They have a similar way of interpreting things. We can more readily relate to them than to others. So we may even feel a sense of cohesion with them and a desire to live close to them. As a result, people with similar values frequently elect to live in the same community.

Our values can serve as guides for our decisions. Some values are of a general nature and permeate many diverse decisions in our lives. Others are very specific.

The following descriptions illustrate how these two sorts of values function.

A friend of mine, Henri, whom I've known since high school, is primarily interested in financial success. In his eyes every lucrative livelihood is good. Henri's been working with computers because this work pays well. But if the computer industry ceases to be a money-making field, he will have no interest in pursuing it. In fact, he's already vowed to leave the field, should that occur.

My cousin Alex, on the other hand, views his computer job quite differently. As a child, he would spend hours playing with old radios, TVs, vacuum cleaners, etc. He always loved tinkering with machinery. Now, as an adult, Alex works with computers primarily because he likes this kind of activity. He relishes the satisfaction he gets from the work itself and intends to continue in this profession for as long as he can and for as long as it remains fulfilling.

Some values have a variety of implications for our lives because they do not refer to specific kinds of actions. When we act on one of these values, different kinds of actions are likely to ensue. Consequently, such values are more difficult to recognize than those whose influence lies in a narrower domain. Let's look at two instances in which values that can affect many diverse activities operate.

My aunt and uncle have always felt that communicating with their children should be a priority. When the children were preteen-agers, the entire family enjoyed biking together. Exploring a bike trail was a good way for them to interact. So they biked together throughout New England. Twenty years later, my aunt and uncle still want to encourage vital interactions within the family. But the children no longer enjoy biking; they have, however, developed an interest in the theatre. So now they go to plays together and chat over dinner. Yes, the activities have changed, but communication within the family has remained a constant value. It continues to influence what this family will do.

My neighbor Margarite's concern for her own physical well-being has led her to engage in a variety of actions. Over the years, she has been interested in doing whatever will be good for her health. Margarite has repeatedly modified her eating and exercise patterns as her knowledge has increased and her health needs have changed. When she was engaged in strenuous sports, for instance, she ate differently than when she became more sedentary in midlife. Now in her 60's, she has changed her diet and exercise regimen again to meet her body's needs and capabilities. The foods Margarite eats today and the activities she participates in are new; but, as always, they have been selected to promote her health.

Most of us find many things worthwhile. We can often discover what is important to us when we notice how we use our free time. Do we talk with a friend? read? go for a run? play with a child? Now then, just as we can choose to read or go running, we can also choose to be ethical.

Being moral is only one of the ways we can act.

Ethical values permeate some people's entire lives. On the other hand, there are individuals in whose character moral values are not deeply imbedded; they act on these values only intermittently or not at all.

• *Do you have a value that affects many of your decisions? What effects has it had on your life?*

When we prize ethical living, we approve of moral action. To act ethically implies deciding not to act in other ways. Very simply, each choice eliminates others.

Ethical actions have different degrees of importance to people. When being moral is integral to the way someone lives his or her whole life, that person will probably not even consider doing something unethical; whereas someone else may be somewhat inclined to act morally, but might not do so when another option seems important. Those who feel attracted to living ethically often find themselves confused. They ask: "What should I do? Should I do the 'right' thing? Or should I do what is easy and convenient? Why should I make this choice and not another?" These are all worthwhile questions. In answering them, we determine what is important to us. When we put our conclusions into practice, our behavior resonates with our values. Our action is imbued with the meaning of our beliefs.

• *Have you ever asked yourself these questions?*
• *If you have, what did you decide to do?*

Your answers are important, for the values you choose deeply influence how you live and who you become.

Let's continue to explore the ways values affect our lives.

Values Have an Impact

First of all, our values affect the way we see things, making some aspects of our experience stand out for us more than others. We tend to notice whatever we have assigned a value. Our values shape our perceptions. Like the lens of a camera, they bring things into focus and enable us to perceive them.

My friend John's behavior is a good illustration of the way values can function. John is outgoing, trim and athletic. As long as I have known him, he has been concerned with his diet. He notices the food he eats: Is it fattening? high in cholesterol? high in fiber? My colleague Li can't understand John at all. Unlike him, she doesn't care about the effects of food on her body. They're unimportant to her. Li allows the whim of the moment to take over and eats whatever she feels like.

We find dynamics parallel to these when we consider ethical actions. Some people are interested in living a moral life. They think through the ethical implications of their choices before acting, while individuals who are not concerned with being ethical never think about their acts in this way.

We are not only affected by the specific values we choose but also by how much we acknowledge them. When we are not sure about what really matters to us, we are likely to be indecisive, drift along with the crowd, feel unsure of ourselves, and have second thoughts about what we're doing.

But when we have our own way of appraising life, we can behave differently. We are more able to choose actions to which we are committed. And we are more likely to be forthright in what we do and how we do it. Our thoughts, feelings, and actions can be congruent.

When we are aware of our own values, we may use them as guides in our everyday lives. For example, some of us choose to join an organization because we want to support its efforts. Others decide to resign from a committee because attending to its concerns is less important than doing something else—such as working for a community group, going to school, taking care of someone they like, or having free time.

Once we know our values, we can prioritize them. After their relative importance is determined, we can know the desirability of each. And we can recognize if one of them in particular is worth more than any of the others.

- *What's important to you?*
- *What's important to your best friend?*
- *What's **most** important to you?*

We Can't Have Everything: Values Compete

People generally embrace many values. Living ethically can be one of them. As soon as we know the importance we give to each of ours, we are able to decide how hard we want to work for its realization. When we deem something "the most important of all," we may more easily determine a direction for our energy and draw up a plan of action.

We are dealing with a different issue, however, when two things are equally important to us, and if doing one of them makes it impossible to do the other. The ensuing conflict cannot be readily resolved. We really can't win! Regardless of what we do—or don't do, we're not going to do something we think is good. This kind of dilemma occurs often. Sometimes, for example, we see it among those who feel equally adamant about adopting ethical values, on the one hand, and promoting their own personal wealth and desires, on the other. They would like to pursue both at the same time, but they can't. This causes an internal struggle or conflict.

Let's look at four situations in which ethical values conflict with other ones.

When Sonja's good friend Sam was in the hospital, he phoned, saying he really wanted to see her that evening. Sonja wanted to visit him and felt she should do so. But how could she? She needed the entire evening to complete a project she had promised her boss for the next day.

My neighbor Nilda began working nine-to-five when her son Adam was five years old. Several weeks into her employment, Nilda realized that she had not played with her son since she began working. Both mother and son missed having fun together. Nilda wanted to relax with her child, yet she also knew she needed to do many household tasks.

My student George wanted to attend medical school. One day, as he was speaking to me about his aspirations, he began to realize he wouldn't be admitted without good grades. After that, he became driven to get them. George hung out with Eric and Luis, two students in his European History class. He recognized that while he excelled in mathematics, they were definitely more proficient in history. Their European History teacher gave the class a project. As George talked about this assignment with Eric and Luis, he felt more and more inclined to use their ideas, which were dazzling and would surely clinch a good grade. But, even though he was tempted to steal his friends' ideas, George firmly believed such behavior was wrong.

My friend Fiona is a teacher, dancer, wife and mother. Her busy life leaves her forever seeking time for herself. Fiona deeply appreciates the beauty of our natural environment. Yet she often feels like dumping her recyclables quickly and easily in with the rest of her garbage. Separating them and taking them to be recycled seem like such a burden to her when time is so scarce.

Sonja, Nilda, George and Fiona ask themselves: "What should I do?"

- *What did you decide to do the last time you were faced with desirable but conflicting options?*
- *Why did you make that choice?*
- *What values does your decision reflect?*

So far we've regarded some of the ways values enter into our lives. Let's now move on to see how two very different kinds of values can affect us—those which are concerned with acquiring possessions and those which reflect caring for people.

Chapter II

ℰℭ

Is There Really a "Loss of Values"?

"Let's Get the Stuff" Takes Over

When people are no longer involved in a religion that stresses moral values, they may grant less importance to its ethical principles. If moral values lose power in people's lives, it becomes easier for other values to take on significance. Advertisers, for instance, can more readily convince some to buy their wares and adopt the life styles which require them.

In the wake of such loss, many develop a passion for things—all kinds of things—a passion which begins to usurp every other concern. Their lives revolve around getting things and having them. Ethical action is of little, if any, interest to them.

Individuals who are so intently focused on having possessions act as if their own well-being is tied directly to acquiring them. Life is thought of as fine when they have many things. It automatically improves when they acquire even more, or bigger, newer, "improved" versions of what they already have. These people believe that the things they have make their lives good.

Clearly, such beliefs are supported by the world of advertising. Sometimes the sales pitch is that we'll be happier if we have bigger, more luxurious things. Automobile advertisements frequently project this message and try to persuade us to want a larger car with a powerful engine. Some individuals go along with these ads and buy such a car, even if only one person is going to drive in it and there will be no opportunity to take advantage of its engine's potential.

Those who believe that acquiring new things is the key to happiness sometimes seek merchandise which is marketed as life-enhancing—that is, more complex, yet smaller and sleeker, than its predecessors. Slimmer, trimmer audio equipment is a case in point. The advertisement implies that life will become as smooth and streamlined as the machinery. Its intricacies will be managed with comparable ease.

People who choose these values disregard moral living. This impacts on us all.

How might they treat us?

Such individuals will often think well of us only when we do or have things with status. We may be esteemed, for instance, because we have many fine possessions and clothes. **Or** perhaps because we go to expensive, fashionable restaurants and eat the "right" foods. **Or** because we live in a good neighborhood. **Or** because we have gone to Ivy League schools and associate with other graduates. **Or** because we have an occupation that is very prestigious or provides us with a substantial income. In every case, the values people embrace affect the the way they live and how they treat others.[2]

The priorities of such individuals vary. Some, for example, may be primarily concerned with the kind of automobile they own, whereas others will focus on the restaurants they frequent or the vacations they take.

- *Do you know anyone who has these kinds of values?*
- *What is most important to them?*
- *How does this affect what they do?*

Of course, individuals who accept only material values have no concern for anything else. For them, even another's well-being bears absolutely no significance. Some will do whatever is necessary to get the things they want. All that matters is owning and having power over things. Other people are worth something only if they can be helpful in this quest. Such an approach to life may ultimately lead them to abuse themselves or others—physically or emotionally—to reach their goals.

At times the possession is a person. When this occurs, people themselves are treated as objects to be owned. The contexts vary. Some may believe that their self-worth comes from having a child, a spouse, a girlfriend, a boyfriend, and so forth. In every case, possessing a person is what counts.

Those who function with this orientation have no concern for nourishing their inner selves. These folks are convinced that there's no need to do so, for their acquisitions alone will transform them and their lives.

- *Look around at those you know—Do any of them manipulate other people as if they were objects?*
- *Has anyone related to you in this way?*
- *How did it feel?*

Can we draw any conclusions from this discussion?

Yes! Let's begin with this: When having possessions and/or wielding power over people are our highest priorities, we are very unlikely to act in an ethical way. Why? Because we do not view persons as valuable in themselves. We are not concerned about avoiding actions that will have negative effects on others or on ourselves. And we never think about doing what is right, only about getting more "stuff."[3]

- *What else can you conclude about this way of living?*

When Other Things are More Important

Now let's look at another group, the "sometimes-caring," who do care about themselves and others, but for whom this is not always the highest priority. The "sometimes-caring" periodically act in a caring way toward people. And from time to time, they act without thinking of the possible effects their behavior could have on others. They might, for example, manipulate someone to get what they want, without even recognizing the harm it inflicts on that person. Yet on many occasions they could, in fact, achieve these same goals without hurting others; but the "sometimes-caring" don't take the time to figure this out.

The "sometimes-caring" are in our midst. One example is the teacher who wants an easy day. This instructor assigns students something pleasant that will occupy them, completely disregarding its lack of educational value. Another situation may include parents who turn their children over to a TV—regardless of what is on—or give them lollipops to keep them quiet. These parents do not consider the other (perhaps long-term) effects of these actions.

Occasionally such callousness comes from a single-minded person with a special talent. He or she could be a musician, a writer, an athlete, or an artist who wants only to perfect a special aptitude; or a business person whose only concern is making money; or a researcher driven to find an answer. Each one is focused solely on a goal and devotes all available energy to it. The intensity of this preoccupation can block out any awareness of the pernicious effects of his or her behavior on other people. Ironically, sometimes these individuals actually believe they're working to benefit others!

- *Look around you—Do you know any people like this?*
- *How have you been treated by them?*
- *How did it feel?*
- *What effect has their way of living had on them?*

Being Ethical is None of the Above

The "sometimes-caring" folks we've just described are not malicious, but neither are they moral. If they were ethical, they would at least be concerned about the welfare of those whom they affect. They would do their best to avoid harming themselves and others. And they might even try to extend themselves to the people in their lives.

Some individuals believe that they are moral when they restrain themselves from particular kinds of acts—such as lying, stealing and cheating—and, conversely, when they always do certain others—such as keeping their promises and telling the truth.[4]

In contrast, there are those who think it's impossible to label some types of acts "always good" or "always bad." They maintain that we can only assess specific individual actions. In other words, to evaluate an act, we need to understand the particular situation in which it is done. Each action's worth is then individually determined by its effects.

When a person chooses to do something because of the positive results it probably will have on the lives of people, that action has an ethical intent.

Those who assess actions in this way differ in their criteria for good effects. Although there are many, several common considerations include: doing no harm to themselves or to others; doing the greatest amount of good for the most people; and doing the most good for all the persons with whom they are involved.[5]

Let us remember here that whenever anything is so important that it precludes concern for people, it is a deterrent to living ethically. A moral person believes all people are valuable and acts accordingly.

This is only one ingredient in moral living.

But it does not answer the following: What characteristics constitute ethical behavior? a moral life? or an ethical person?

These questions elude simple responses. After centuries of debate, there's no agreement in sight. Yet it is possible to glean a family of characteristics from the answers we have.[6]

Let's look at them now.

Chapter III

✻

Moral Persons and Ethical Acts

Feelings Are the Foundation

Throughout Western history moral actions have been thought of as those which impact upon people. Today, many extend this definition to encompass those acts which affect the environment, animals and beautiful objects.

Should we also consider these kinds of actions ethical? That's for you to answer. But for the purposes of this discussion, let's limit ourselves to those actions that are most often considered moral—namely, actions which directly affect people.

Recently I heard someone say: "Vivian's ethical. She does what's right." This wasn't surprising. I know Vivian well. She is ethical. When given a choice, she does good things. Yet this alone does not make her ethical. Vivian is ethical—not merely because of what she does—but because of the way in which she does it.

When Vivian acts, she is aware of what she's doing. Her action is driven by the conviction that it's good to do what is right. Responsibility is felt and accepted. Vivian genuinely cares about what she does. In acting morally, she manifests honesty and courage.

An ethical action has many facets. It entails knowledge and awareness, an effort to do what is good, an acceptance of responsibility, and feelings of respect and caring. Together, these aspects contribute to making an action moral. When we live ethically for some time, we become integrated and our ability to be moral grows stronger.

Feelings play a critical role in ethical action. Our sentiments are a source of moral acts and remain one of their essential elements. Moreover, an action can be considered ethical *only* if moral feelings are present. What kinds of feelings are they? There are those akin to caring—for one's self as well as for others.[7] There's love and respect for the truth. And there's courage to follow one's own convictions.

Not everyone accepts the idea that feelings are important in moral action. There are diverse opinions on this subject. Some philosophers, such as David Hume,[8] have explicitly recognized the place of feelings. Others never refer to them. Instead, they address a variety of moral issues without mentioning feelings—as if these were irrelevant to moral behavior.[9] Unlike the ideas espoused by this last group, my interpretation of ethical acts gives feelings a pivotal role. (The reasons for my position will be explained later.) To me the foundation of moral behavior consists of: respecting others, caring about them, being concerned with the effects of our actions on those involved, being sufficiently knowledgeable and brave to act in their best interest, and doing so because we believe it is right.

- *Whom do you care about?*
- *How does it feel when you act on their behalf?*
- *Look around—do you know anyone who says and does good things but doesn't seem to care about people?*
- *What do you think of this cavalier attitude?*

Moral feelings vary in intensity. Sometimes they seem to be more like concern than caring, whereas at other times they are close to loving.

In all instances, a feeling of caring can arise only under certain conditions. As a precondition for its occurrence, we must attend to other people and become aware of their separate existence and unique identity. Then we not only know about them, but also genuinely hear them, see them, and feel their presence. We experience them as something marvelous, and we take delight in this awareness. Their very existence is appreciated.[10]

When we perceive others in this way, we are likely to sense our shared humanity. We all become fellow travellers in this life. No separation is felt between the experience of "me" and "them." A sense of "we" emerges. Then we may begin to feel for them and care about them. Feeling this way toward others, while realizing that they are like ourselves, has been called *empathy*. It underlies the ethical principle, "Do unto others as you would have them do unto you." And it serves as a foundation for moral action.[11]

- *When do you feel this kind of connectedness?*
- *How do you get yourself to act on behalf of others when you don't experience them in this way?*

Let's pause to take stock in what's been said here.

Living ethically requires several important elements: knowledge of what we are doing; feelings of concern for the persons involved in our decisions; goals that consider their well-being; a commitment to these purposes; and the courage to realize them. Moreover, when we act in this way, we become whole—for our mind, spirit and body are working together.

Right and Wrong Acts

Now we'll consider how ethical action is generally understood in Western culture. What are its most widely recognized characteristics?

First of all, as we've just noted, the motives propelling ethical actions distinguish them from other actions. When people act morally, they want to do what is right. Moreover, they want to be kind to others as well as to themselves. So they are mindful of the impact their actions may have on people. As a result, being ethical requires an openness to, a sensitivity for, and an understanding of people.

Circumstances play a role in determining the specific goal of an ethical action and the effects it can achieve. In ideal times moral people are able to increase human well-being. But on other occasions they may only be able to avoid hurting people. In still tougher situations the best anyone can do is cause the least harm. For then all available avenues of action entail negative repercussions. The best choice in such predicaments has the least undesirable consequences.

In the worst scenario, ethical action is the path least harmful to people; and in the best circumstances, it is the most beneficial one.

If you're still with me, dear reader, let's go on to explore still another way of understanding right and wrong acts.

Throughout history some people have earmarked certain kinds of acts as "always right" and others as "always wrong." When we have clear guidelines such as these, right and wrong can be readily communicated. And ethical decision-making is simplified.

Telling the truth and keeping promises, for example, have long been considered "right" actions. Lying, stealing, cheating, or harming others have been consistently labelled "wrong." With this kind of clarity "right" actions can be encouraged and warnings can be raised against "wrong" ones. Praise and punishment are meant to foster good behavior. The purpose is to protect people from each other and to promote trust among them.

When a person is deciding to do a "right" act rather than a "wrong" one, the motive can be to avoid punishment or to preserve one's own reputation. Acting in this way may not be bad, but it is not moral. Why? Because there is no desire here to do what's best—for others as well as for one's self.

Some view the labelling of certain acts as "right" and others as "wrong" merely as guidelines, not hard-and-fast rules. They believe that a policy of doing those so-called "good acts" and always refraining from the "bad ones" is not always best. Julie is a good example. On one occasion Julie made a point of telling her ailing friend Anne how lovely she looked—even though it wasn't true. Julie later confided in me that she was actually concerned about Anne's pallor but thought it best to cheer her up. Julie does not like to lie; yet she thought it better to lie to Anne at that time. Julie believes that the worth of a specific action can only be determined within its context. For her the effects of her actions on people is the decisive factor.

Like Julie, many people maintain that the right choice is always the one that will do good things for people. Those who've accepted this route sometimes find themselves in disagreement with each other. They debate over such issues as: How much should we try to do for others? To whom should we extend ourselves? Why? How should we balance the benefits we seek for ourselves with those we pursue for others?

Whenever we try to realize the most good, we repeatedly see we cannot do everything that would be helpful to everyone. We are faced with difficult choices. So then we may ask ourselves: What should we do? How do we decide the best thing to do? How can we give just consideration to the needs and rights of everyone involved?

Yes, when we're concerned about the effects of our actions on several people, questions of fairness do arise. And when we feel a genuine desire to be fair, we are clearly interested in promoting the quality of human life.

- *Have you found yourself faced with issues like these when interacting with your friends, family, children, employees, or fellow workers?*
- *How did you respond?*

Hollow People Can Look Good

It can be difficult to determine whether someone is acting morally or not. An act that at first glance seems ethical on closer scrutiny can prove to be unethical, because it does not stem from moral intentions.

To clarify this, I'd like to tell you about Jim. Deception, lying and petty thievery are a way of life for him. But at times Jim has told the truth—for example, when he had something to gain or when a lie would be easily discovered. One time Jim even admitted that he restrained himself from altering his employer's books to get extra money for himself. "Quite frankly," he said, "I would have been found out."

Jim's actions certainly were socially acceptable. And he appeared to be ethical when he told the truth. When Jim refrained from stealing, he really did nothing wrong. He even seemed to be an honest person. Yet his actions were merely a way of serving his own interests. Any benefit derived by others was purely accidental. Jim possessed absolutely no concern for them or for doing what is right.

We find a comparable situation whenever government officials support legislation to increase their popularity with voters. Sometimes with their efforts bills are passed that will help improve their constituents' lives. Eventually, however, the voters may realize that some of these politicians don't care about such measures. The legislation these individuals backed was promoted only to secure votes and greater political power.

- *Have you witnessed people—politicians, members of a school board, judges, or friends—change their positions on an issue when it was advantageous for them?*
- *How did you view them afterwards?*

It's also common to see parents engage in covert self-serving behavior. Mary and Gene are a prime example. By dressing their children in beautiful clothing, taking them on vacations and providing them with toys, they hope to be viewed as good parents. Their main concern, however, is their own reputation. In spite of such motives, their children have indeed benefited. Mary and Gene are, in fact, responsible for making some good things happen. But we cannot say that these parents are kind, generous or considerate with respect to their children.

- *Do you know parents who, for self-serving reasons, provide clothes, toys, music lessons, or private schooling for their children?*
- *What do you think of their behavior?*

Sometimes immoral people work arduously for an organization founded to improve life. The group's goal may be to combat poverty, homelessness, inadequate education, malnutrition, or the deteriorating environment. These unethical persons may even talk about wanting to make the world a better place. But their actions are motivated by any number of other reasons. For example, they may be trying to hide a self-serving agenda: some may hope to convince others to like them by projecting a favorable image of themselves.

Most people want to look as if they mean well and therefore conduct themselves to create that impression. Some are so good at this, it's difficult to determine if they're truly ethical or not. Their tone of voice and recurring smile can create an illusion of kindness and friendliness. They may also talk about how they want to do what is right and how they have tried to help others. When such people also occasionally do something beneficial to others, it's easy to be fooled.

The point here is a simple one. The words, gestures, and actions of these people are hollow. Their visible behavior does not reflect their intentions. Hollow people act out a charade. They feel no concern for anyone else. So when "appearing to be ethical" no longer pays off, they abandon it to serve their own interests.

Morality or Self-Interest?

Now let's address a common misconception. I've known many people who have come to believe that we either watch out for ourselves or act ethically. They think that being moral always entails losing. This view is prevalent among those who believe everyone else is at odds with them and may be a competitor. Such individuals are prone to think: "I either take care of myself or them. I can't do both."

But clearly this is not the only way to understand our relationship to others. As a matter of fact, if we experience ourselves as similar to other human beings, as co-existing in this life with them, and as sharing common concerns, we're apt to think otherwise. Then, whenever we consider doing something for ourselves, we're also likely to reflect on what our action might do to them.

This point of view is *essential* for ethical action.

We can get an insight into our perspective on other people by noticing how we feel when we avoid hurting them, or when we protect and help them.

- *Think of certain people you know.*
- *How do you feel when you're expected to do something for them?*
- *Is it an inconvenience?*
- *Does it feel like an intrusion or do you enjoy helping them?*
- *And do you like seeing their lives improve?*

As people live, their perceptions and the things they take pleasure in change. Individuals develop throughout their lives in a variety of ways. We have already considered two radically different kinds of evolution. At one extreme are people who experience unrelenting competition with others and who view their own concerns as always in conflict with the interests of others. In sharp contrast are other individuals who do not feel isolated and at odds with everyone else.

We develop our own selves by the way we live. The thoughts, feelings, values and actions we adopt are important in making decisions. They influence how we use our natural abilities and other resources. Through our choices, we shape our lives and our selves.[12] The kind of person we become is largely up to us.

We always have the option to ignore, to adopt, or to reject opportunities for becoming moral. Ethical action and moral character, however, remain available to us. By living ethically, we develop the perceptions, attitudes, and feelings of a moral person. This, of course, will only happen if we choose it.

By examining the roles values play in our lives, we can learn more about being moral.

Let's explore this further.

PART TWO

LIVING MORALLY: DIFFICULTIES AND DETERRENTS

Chapter IV

ॐ

Ethical Values

How Could We Live with Them?

Values play a central role in our lives. With them we can more easily know what we want to do. For if we do not have them, we would be equally interested in, or indifferent to, everything. Like a ship without a rudder, we would go along aimlessly.

Most people do not live without values. Yet I hear distressing complaints about the "loss of values" or the "lack of values."

What do these remarks mean?

It strikes me that most often these critics are really saying people are not living ethically but have instead given in to societal pressures. Quite frequently these immoral people have adopted the values regularly expressed in the media. This is not at all surprising. Magazines, television, popular music, the movies and the internet have now become the strongest voices in our society. And they have been feeding the populace a steady stream of beliefs and values which are similar to those found in advertisements.

To be ethical, we must counteract these ever present forces. The struggle is not always easy. And it's certainly not a new one. Since the earliest days of Western civilization, people have been faced with societal elements that could undermine moral life.

On the other hand, throughout history people have also advocated those values and ways of interpreting the world which support an ethical life (as we can see in chapter IX). The cornerstones of such a life are: regarding ourselves and others as having inherent worth, and valuing our inner selves. Moreover, those who believe in moral living often think that our inner life makes us human and renders each of us unique. When someone adopts these views, every person is considered valuable; respect and protection are due to all; and every form of prejudice and racism is appalling.

Ethical values are revealed, for example, when people talk of human rights and strive to protect them; when they speak of the value of each person's freedom and work to ensure it; and when they respect the privacy of others and protect their friendships. [13]

How can we account for the prevalence of ethical values in the evolution of Western culture?

First of all, we can trace evidence of continuity from the people of one generation to the next and from one civilization to another, dating back to the ancient Hebrews, the early Christians, and the Greco-Roman civilizations. Christianity and Judaism became the primary torchbearers of Western civilization's values. (We will consider their influence in chapter IX.)

These two religions express certain moral precepts which can provide guidance for ethical living. When the followers of a religion live by its moral teachings, the relationship between these moral values and being religious is very apparent.

Today, the connection between ethical values and religion is often weak or even nonexistent. There are at least two explanations for this. First, many people do not have strong religious ties. And secondly, some religious leaders do not exemplify the very humanistic values they preach. By living hypocritically, they have betrayed the trust of their followers. So their example cannot serve as a model for ethical living.

In spite of these factors, a belief in human worth has had a profound influence on many. Indeed, this long, venerable tradition in Western culture impresses itself upon us profoundly through the people and institutions that embody it.

How do we attain values?

Most often we are not aware of our values or of how we have acquired them. Values are communicated to us throughout our lives from many different sources. As we've already observed, they are expressed by the models of behavior portrayed in the media. For the most part, however, we learn values from a very early age by just living with those who embrace them.

Ways of interpreting and organizing experience are acquired in part by merely living and communicating with others. By interacting with our parents and families, as well as with our friends and teachers, we have learned how to talk about our lives and experiences and thereby how to understand and evaluate them. Strategies for coping with life are passed from one person to the next, and from each generation to successive ones.[14]

Sometimes teachers, youth-group leaders (such as in the Girl Scouts and Boy Scouts), our parents and other family members, religious leaders, and others bring the values they espouse to our attention.

- *Has anyone made you aware of your values?*
- *Do you know who or what has influenced your choice of values?*

Let's continue to look at the process of acquiring values, for I'd like to make a few other points.

We've just noticed some of the influences in our midst which can affect our values. But this account is not meant to project the idea that we've all been thoroughly programmed. To the contrary! We are not merely pawns in our environment. The ways of others become our own *only* when we choose to adopt them. The various contexts in which we live do not alone determine our values or whom we will follow. But they surely have the power to offer us alternatives. And that they certainly do!

As children, we may decide to pattern ourselves after a person—such as a favorite relative, a teacher, a friend's parents—or a character we encounter in a movie, a TV program or a book. In addition to selecting our role models, we can, as we mature, also choose from an array of life styles. And we then have the option of replacing our chosen way of life with another. Unfortunately, some people are not aware of their capacity to make such choices. Yet once we recognize this ability, we can begin to guide our lives more effectively.

- *Whom have you chosen to emulate?*
- *Why have you chosen this person?*

Certainly, much more can be said about making choices. So it's important to reconsider this later.

Now, it's interesting to note that once we acquire values, we're usually unaware of living with them. They become an integral part of the way we live, one of our habits of thinking. They feel "natural" to us. Like habits, values can directly and indirectly affect the way we live. And they can impact on the way we behave while we remain unaware of their influence.[15]

Before we go on to other topics, let's see how far we've come. We've seen that the values underlying an ethical life are prevalent in Western culture today side by side with values that are very different from them. There are people who live in mindful consideration of others and there are those who are only concerned with the material conditions of their own lives. Adopting either of these approaches to life results in different actions.

- *What effects do these contrasting influences have on you?*

Making Decisions: What Should I Do?

The process of making decisions that are right for us is complex. At the start we can reflect on what gives us satisfaction. For in order to do what we believe is best, we need not only to understand the available options but also to know their value for us. Yet, even with knowledge of the things we would like to do, our decision may not be readily forthcoming—especially if we have wide interests and limited time.

Determining which option is most important to us, however, will not necessarily indicate a route for action. We still need a method of realizing our priorities in the situation at hand and time to reflect on the people and circumstances involved. Then with a greater understanding of the given context, we may be better able to decide the best way of achieving our goal. The decision-making process takes both time and effort.

Now a decision of this sort, at best, gives us only a realistic "game plan." Nothing happens unless we act on these notions. And action occurs only if our convictions are sufficiently strong. When our ideas challenge us to act in ways that are unusual for us or in a manner not readily accepted by others, courage may be required.

To sum up: living according to our values is a complex matter requiring reflection, knowledge, consideration, conviction and, at times, courage.

The process of becoming clear on the choices we want to make and acting on them is complicated by our culture, which frequently impresses contrasting values upon us. As we very well know, diverse values vie for our acceptance. There are those that promote an ethical life and those that do not: A respect for people and a concern for their well-being are juxtaposed with a desire to have power over people and a willingness to use them (including ourselves) to achieve goals. As we select our thoughts and actions, the presence of these two sets of values can generate inner turmoil.

What might happen when we try to adopt both kinds of values?

The least troublesome scenario is the one in which we can strive for both with some hope of success. Careers which are personally satisfying, provide services for others, and are lucrative as well are a case in point.

But jobs that fulfill all these criteria are rare. Many occupations (such as nursing, teaching, and social work) that are often personally rewarding do not usually command high salaries. And many careers that often pay well (stock brokering and investment banking, for example) do not always provide an opportunity for personal fulfillment.

Our choice is truly a difficult one when the options at each pole seem equally desirable. Then we're likely to feel torn between the alternatives. We experience a conflict in values. Which should we choose?

But if the choices available do not mean much to us, the clash is not very formidable. You may even find yourself wondering—Do I really want to go after any of this?

- *Have you ever experienced conflict between personal fulfillment and financial success?*
- *How did you resolve it?*
- *Do you know anyone who's made a different kind of decision in a comparable situation?*

New Technology

Sometimes a choice does involve competing values, but having to choose between them is not necessarily the source of the challenge we experience. Instead, we can encounter difficulty simply from the newness of a situation. Because we are not used to dealing with it, we may not be clear about what avenues are open to us. And once we discover them, we may not know much about their implications.

Such is often the case when new technology is involved. It permits us to do things we've never done before, or never even thought of doing! For example, we now have astonishing ways of intervening in life to ameliorate physical disorders. And we also can extend the life of a person in ways that fifty years ago could only have been dreamt of. Power of this magnitude is at times exhilarating.

But if we try to make a decision in the face of new technology, we may very well feel bewildered. Such confusion is likely to occur, especially when we haven't tacitly adopted the mind-set that whatever is new is always better. Consequently, when we face a choice of medical treatments, the latest procedures, devices, or medications are not necessarily the best route to go. The fact that they are new is not in itself a good enough reason to use them.

The situation is further complicated when we want to treat a sick person with respect. Then we can't just pick a treatment option that will merely help the ailment; we must also be sure it will fit in with the life choices of the patient. The decision is very complex. With ever-changing technology, we may very well not know anyone else who's faced these specific alternatives. But even if we do know of someone, the issues need to be thought out anew for each patient. There are no set guidelines. What should we do? We are left with the task of figuring this out for ourselves.

To clarify matters, let's consider the following situation. My cousins and I have been concerned about our elderly relative, Aunt Jenny. She has lived with diabetes for many years, and complications have set in with old age.

The first thing we discovered was that there are many methods of treatment. Should we try drugs? If so, which ones? A new procedure? Or perhaps a combination of procedures and drugs? What would Jenny want to do? We soon realized that we couldn't begin to decide unless we first answered the questions buzzing through our heads: What can each one of these options do by itself or in concert with another? What side effects can be anticipated? What are the chances for success? How might each option change Jenny's life? Will she think it is good to live that way? What are the risks? Does Jenny think it is worth it?

As you can see, there were no obvious answers and no clear-cut solutions. To make a good decision, we needed to assess every alternative—not only in terms of its effectiveness as a procedure, but also for its effects on our aunt's physical and emotional well-being. Moreover, as always, there was uncertainty: no one could predict the outcomes.

Instead of getting involved with all this, it would have been easier and less worrisome for us just to accept the newest procedure. And if we took this route, we were likely to reap an additional benefit—to be respected by those who trust technology to make life better. If favorable recognition by these people were our goal, this course of action would have worked. But this is not where we were coming from. We were concerned about Aunt Jenny and knew that a wrong decision on our part could create terrible consequences for her.

We soon realized there was another way to circumvent all these difficulties. We could just ask her physicians for their recommendations. Finding reputable specialists in diabetes and relying solely on their judgment are considered responsible tacks to take. By following the advice of specialists, we would be generally viewed as having done our best. We could then take refuge behind the prestige of these physicians.

But we cared about Jenny, so we asked ourselves: Do any of these specialists know what Jenny would want? Can physicians make the best decisions without having asked her? Our answer to both these questions was—No. These doctors had just met our aunt the previous week, when they had been called in on the case because her medications no longer kept her body in balance. None had known Jenny as a friend. How could they have? They had only spent a few minutes with her.

- *Do you ever rely on someone with expert knowledge?*
- *How do you make use of this person's advice?[16]*

The point here is that selecting the latest method of treatment simply because it's new or relying blindly on the judgment of an expert are fairly facile ways to make a decision. But choices arrived at in this manner are not ethical. If we consider the requisite factors for moral action, we can see how ethical decision-making differs from this behavior.

To help us better understand these two ways of making choices, let's look at the necessary elements in moral action: First we need to know our own values. We also need to be sensitive to the people and situations involved, and to develop an understanding of them. Patience also is required for sifting through relevant information. And, finally, courage enables us to make our own decisions. This decision-making process, as we noted earlier, always takes time and effort. Moreover, to determine what is best in a situation like Aunt Jenny's demands a great deal of both.

We've already recognized some of the prevalent practices and approaches to living that can diminish our ability to recognize our own values as well as our capacity to act on them. And furthermore, we know that when we succumb to any of them, we are simultaneously deterred from being moral.

Let's now examine some other factors which can undermine ethical action.

Chapter V

૭૦૦૪

"To Be or Not to Be":
Deterrents to Ethical Action

W e can choose to act ethically or decide not to. Moral actions are different from those things that happen accidentally, like bumping into someone. And they don't occur unexpectedly, like inadvertently running into a friend while on vacation. Instead, we will be ethical only if we *decide* that we *want* to be and take steps to act accordingly.

In other words, we can't be indifferent to how we're living and be ethical. Indifference, in fact, is a major deterrent. To be moral, we must really want to live ethically, and we have to consciously choose to do so.

We must perceive ourselves as having the energy to propel our own actions. And we need to trust ourselves, believing that we can indeed act in the best possible ways. These views, attitudes and beliefs, however, will not by themselves make us ethical. We also have to respect, appreciate and value human beings.

From this vantage point, it becomes apparent that some of the ingredients necessary for ethical action are: the desire to be ethical, the ability to tap our energies to pursue this goal, and the *felt* appreciation for the supreme value of all people.

Whatever can deprive us of these necessary elements also undermines our capacity to be ethical.

Let's consider one of these components: the ability to harness our energies to live ethically—because many societal conditions can erode our sense of self-power, personal uniqueness, and self-worth.

Here are some of them.

"Drifters"

At times certain people we find around us are debilitating. Particularly draining are those who seem to live without any values of their own. These folks are seemingly innocuous, but their presence can have a negative effect on us.

Let me explain. The people I'm thinking of have no definite idea of what's important to them. The phrase "there is a loss of values" genuinely applies to them. They live without any values in mind. Their behavior does not stem from within themselves. Instead, the pushes and pulls from the society around them determine what they do. They are all too ready to follow the advice and recommendations of others. At work these folks generally carry out the orders of their superiors without hesitation. They never stop to question the directives themselves.

Moreover, when advertising claims announce that the newest product is good for them, these individuals have no reason to ask whether or not it is actually worthwhile. It is new. It is fashionable. They've been told this makes it desirable and they should want it; so they do. When people respond this way, their behavior does not originate from their own values and decisions. Consequently, they often live *half-heartedly*. And when they function only in this mode, they are *unable* to act ethically.[17]

Like any other human conduct, however, this manner of living sets an example for others. Unless we are sure of our own selves, the very presence of "drifters" could lead us to question our own decisiveness and may generate feelings of uncertainty. Moreover, when we allow their way of living to become ours, we are deterred from acting ethically.

- *Do you know any "drifters?"*
- *How do you feel when you're with them?*

What You See Is What You Get

Some factors in society can erode other facets of being moral—namely, our capacity to be autonomous agents and our ability to be respectful of persons. For instance, pressure exists within some socio-economic groups to live up to certain notions of prestige. As a result, those people who desire social status within a particular group may permit its ideals to heavily influence their selection of housing, schooling and professional life. No thought is given to the impact of these choices on any of the persons involved. The status seekers merely want to fulfill the requirements for group approval.

In a similar vein, messages conveyed by mass media and advertising frequently encourage us to go along with trends and just be followers. To some extent, these savvy marketeers have even made it seem pointless for us to make our own decisions.

Why are these media messages so successful? For a start—they're clever. And the means are indirect. So they can influence us when we're not expecting it.

One such advertising ploy has been to communicate the notion that our image is the most important thing in the world. These advertisements bombard the public with: wear these jeans, these sunglasses, this shirt, this cologne . . . and, above all else, be sexy! By emphasizing this idea *ad infinitum*, promotional material locates our worth and identity in our outer shell. These messages are so pervasive that some people are even convinced that our appearance is all there is. They believe the adage "What you see is what you get!"

This point of view ignores—even denies—that we have the capacity to make our own decisions.

Sometimes, however, the media's messages appear to be different. They communicate something comparable to "Wear this and you'll be an individual." The explicit goal here is to be your own person. That seems to be on the right track. But, while supporting autonomy, these advertisements simultaneously undermine it by demanding passivity: "Accept the dictates of this ad. Follow its directives. Change your appearance and thereby become the author of your own decisions."

Teen-agers and young adults—perhaps more than any other segment of society—strive to establish their individuality through adornments such as clothing, jewelry, and body paint. They do everything in their power to avoid established practices. And these young people quite often succeed.

Nevertheless, flaunting of convention does not make them "their own person." For in abiding by society's emphasis on outward appearances, they've only succeeded in looking different.

This way of thinking is also found in other contexts. As an example, those who exhort us to enter a particular profession and thereby become a significant person are saying in effect, "Attach credentials to your name and you will become a better person." Although they're focusing on our professional identity rather than on our physical appearance, their approach to us is the same.

- *The next time you look at a magazine, newspaper or the TV, notice the underlying messages conveyed in the commercials and print ads.*
- *Think about the people you know. Do any of them think that they are "better" because of the things they've attached to themselves?*

People who accept these messages are swept away in the prevailing tides of society. They float through life disconnected from their own desires. They're not following the beat of their own drummer. How can they? They can't hear it and don't even know how to listen to it.[18]

Physical Fitness

Physical fitness programs are another way to attend to appearances. Engaging in exercise may seem at first glance to reflect a concern for self-development. Yet the focus is just as likely to be on the workout clothing, the image created while doing the activities, the status involved in being able to afford it, and the way one's body looks to others once it is toned. Thus the inherent pleasures and rewards of the activities themselves may go unnoticed.

As each new fad replaces the last, some people flit from one kind of physical activity to another, while others adhere to trends in personal adornment and consumer goods.

Physical activities can be a diversion from life's main issues. Participating in strenuous exercise may provide a temporary escape, but it does not address any of the issues—such as housing, finances, personal relationships and so forth—that need attention.

No one will deny that physical exercise can bring about a "high" and provide a feeling of well-being. But when people begin exercising solely to impress others or to retreat from life, these effects rapidly wear off. Consequently, there's a recurring need to create a patina of feeling good.

Let's briefly review what we've just talked about.

All the strategies discussed in this chapter (such as following the directives of others, focusing on appearances, and creating a physical "high") deal only with the surface of life. When people live exclusively with such activities, they ignore the possibility of having an inner self with its own self-fulfilling values. The thought of guiding themselves with their own values is unlikely to arise.

To be sure, the modes of conduct just considered always preclude adhering to our own beliefs. Our inner self is not necessarily denied; it is just ignored. As a result, our ability to relate to an inner self and to live vibrantly through it is weakened. And our capacity for living morally is undermined.

As we've recently noticed, those who look to others for direction are most likely to ignore their own inner selves. They seek guidelines on how to look, what to have and what to do. The results of opinion polls and the comments expressed in critical reviews, for instance, are accepted as gospel truth. The tacit belief throughout is: I shall discover what to think by asking others. And when they tell me, I should heed their words.

People who shape their lives in response to others are readily swayed. When those from whom they want approval expect something else, the acceptance seekers promptly begin to feel that they themselves should change.

- *Look around: Do you see anyone trying to persuade others?*
- *Who is looking for direction?*

Competition: It's Me or You

Our ability to act ethically can also be undermined by the very people from whom we seek guidance. For they may understand us only in relationship to others. By perceiving us, others and our relationships comparatively, they can indirectly communicate that all people are rivals. Yes, it's important to look at the competitiveness implied, for it may influence our perceptions and, in turn, our ability to appreciate human beings. Moreover, this orientation can diminish our capacity for making our own decisions. In short, it can have a negative impact on moral living.

Let's explore this further.

To begin, once we adopt a contentious point of view, everyone appears to be striving to be better than everyone else. And so it is easy to get caught up in seeing ourselves only as we measure up to others. This mode of living offers no way of gaining a sense of autonomy.

The ever present goal here—to be better than—can take on a life of its own. When it does, no thought is given to whether a particular success is worth having: winning is sought for its own sake. We don't expect ourselves to think of what we want to be or do. Having values of our own is irrelevant.

Since a competitive point of view affects how we perceive others, it often influences how we treat them. Once we adopt this orientation, we reduce others to either our inferiors or our superiors. Their comparative worth provides a rationale for believing that we have a right to rule over them, or that we must be subservient. When we allow ourselves only these alternatives, there's no room for appreciating our competitors for who they are.

This way of understanding people permeates much of our schooling. The pervasive grading-testing system ranks people, setting the stage for competitive personal interactions. And the authoritative, condescending role assumed by some teachers and administrators projects an image of a hierarchy among people.

A majority of children in many societies spend the greater part of their waking hours in schools. The orientation commonly found in these environments can be deeply ingrained in children during their most formative years. Once a way of perceiving one's self and others is established in the young, it is relatively easy for society to sustain it in adults. This point is critical to our concerns here. For when schools engender feelings of competitiveness in students, they are molding young people who are likely to have little difficulty with unethical behavior. A combative approach toward others is, in fact, incompatible with living ethically.

Let's see why this is so.

If we view people as competitive with us, we see them as always ready to take advantage of a situation to become better than we. Such an attitude can very well lead us to feel that we should become self-protective. In response, we are likely to take on a defensive posture or an active competitive stance, in an effort to protect ourselves from their power or to become "more" than they. We may unwittingly strive to diminish their capacities by witholding information, goods, services, or affection. We may even devise overt ways of undermining them. In any case, as rivals, we are unlikely to look out for our opponents' well-being. To be kind, considerate, or generous for their sake just might give them an advantage.

Some people live their entire lives competitively. They always relate this way. The specific context in which they find themselves isn't even taken into account. Little thought, if any, is given to the worthiness of the endeavors at hand or to the effects they could produce. As a result, their actions can very well alienate the others involved and even prove stressful and distasteful to themselves. None of this is considered. Now, on the other hand, if these people were to reflect on their own behavior, they could author their actions in another way. They could stop being pawns for their habits of mind.

In sharp contrast to those who mindlessly live out ingrained habits are the "whistle blowers." These individuals have not been subdued into indifference or apathy. An impulse to protect themselves does not dominate their lives. They'll even risk their own economic and social well-being when something more important is at stake. They have a strong sense of their own values and a willingness to act on them. Their desire to prevent something bad from happening and their determination to do what they believe is right override all other considerations.

Before going on, let's think for a moment about what's just been said. We've looked at numerous modes of living that preclude being ethical. Each serves as a way of understanding and responding to ourselves, to others, and to the world. The insidious factor here is that they are self-perpetuating. They usually do not completely destroy us; they simply render our lives hollow.

- *The question we need to ask ourselves is: Do I just want to subsist or do I want to live a satisfying life?*

If the quality of our lives is important to us, then it is in our own best interest to know which aspects of our society promote unethical ways of living. Fortunately, when we are aware of life-diminishing elements and the effects they can have on us, we can become impervious to them.

So let's consider some other deterrents to ethical living.

Chapter VI

ଜ୍ଞଓଃ

Experts Don't Always Help!

E xperts exercise a strong influence over people today. Many of us look to psychologists, psychiatrists, sociologists and other professionals to discover how to understand ourselves and others.

These professionals provide us with ideas about human nature and the dynamics of human change. When we accept any of these approaches, we have a ready-made guide for interpreting experience.

Authorities do us a great service by providing ways of sorting, organizing and speaking about our experiences. And because of their wide acceptance, they give us a way of communicating about our selves which can be readily understood. But this does not mean that their ideas necessarily stimulate us to create our own interpretations of our selves. On the contrary. Their ideas are often easy to use and can, in fact, promote passive acceptance.

The perspective adopted by these experts often projects the impression that patterns for our behavior do exist and that the shape of our lives arises from the circumstances in which we have been living.

To the extent that we go along with such ideas, we permit them to affect our capacity to think for ourselves, to determine our own values, and to be moral. That is why I want to examine this way of thinking with you.

People, especially those working as professionals, often view us through a variety of classifications—such as our skin color, sex, age, ethnic background, years of formal education, the way we have performed on certain tests, where we live, our religion, the number of siblings in our family and our place among them. Untold numbers of charts and statistical tables have been developed to illustrate the characteristics of the members of each group and the typical behavior found within it. To illustrate this point, let's turn our attention to books about children. In these works categorizations frequently determine the topic of concern—the stages of development, the gifted child, the learning-disabled child, the only child, and the middle child, etc.

Surely there are numerous classifications for us all. With each we are understood only in so far as we fit into a particular category. Some people try to discover the groups into which they can be placed so that they will better understand their own salient features.

- *How might you be classified?*
- *In what respects have classifications helped you understand yourself and others?*
- *When and in what ways are they not illuminating?*

The descriptions formulated by these professionals imply that the circumstances of our lives (our natural endowments, as well as the existing physical, social, and economic conditions) are critical factors in molding us. The impression often created is that once these conditions are known, they can be used to explain the course of our life thus far and to describe what we are most likely to do. The expected behavior is then considered normal for us.

Many take this to mean that when a person lives out a norm, "everything's O.K." Adherents of such beliefs may even come to think that they themselves ought to reflect such standards and strive to be "well-adjusted." The tacit message is that people can change—but should do so only within the scope of what is considered normal. The norm serves not only as the goal but also as the limit for behavior.

Whenever we accept this point of view, we see ourselves as having been shaped by what has happened to us and, consequently, as likely to behave in a certain manner. Circumstances appear to propel us. Our behavior seems to be a spin-off from the context of our lives. As a result, many of us assume that we are not responsible for ourselves.

The explanations proffered by these experts can help us recognize the things we have in common with others and the significance these elements could have for us. But let us also keep in mind that these accounts do not necessarily present the whole picture. In fact, very often the possibility of self-initiated action and self-generated energy is missing. Should this occur, there's little recognition of our ability to make unique interpretations and to have our own particular reactions to experiences. Needless to say, when professionals overlook these abilities, they also fail to mention that there are no rules for our responses.

To be sure, the point here is that these professionals do not necessarily *intend* to deny the possibility of personal decisions. They often just ignore it and generate convincing ways to account for us and our world without ever referring to individual initiative. With this one omission, however, it is much *easier* to overlook the fact that we *can* influence the direction of our own life.

So the orientation of these experts can deter us from looking to our own selves as a source of our own desires and actions. For once we place the origin of action *outside* our selves, we define our selves as reactors, not actors—as receivers, not shapers. And then we take no responsibility for whatever occurs. Instead, we're likely to blame the situations and people in our lives for what we ourselves have done and who we've become. In locating all power in external conditions, we turn ourselves into victims. And we rob ourselves of our own ability to be ethical.[19]

- *Do you know people who blame their parents, the circumstances of their early life, their spouse, or their children for why they live as they do?*
- *Do you know others who do* **not** *look solely outside of themselves to account for their lives?*
- *Do you notice anything that happens to people when they view themselves in each of these ways?*

Once again, we've seen that the way others define us and the expectations they have for us are forces in our lives. What we do in response to these perceptions, however, determines their significance for us.

We can, on the one hand, blindly accept them and thereby weaken our capacity for self-determination. Or we can place ourselves in the driver's seat. We might then realize that when we let others define us, an essential element has been omitted: namely, that we can live our *own* lives in response to our *own* beliefs, values, and ideals. By adopting this self-affirming point of view, we are more likely to use the valuable insights of professionals, or anyone else whom we trust, for interpreting experience and for making ethical choices—*without* relinquishing our place at the helm. Living with this perspective is a prerequisite for being moral.

PART THREE

ETHICS:
A "YES" TO LIFE

Chapter VII

ℰℭ

Living With or Without Your Own Values

A Life With Meaning

In the preceding chapters, we have considered three building blocks of moral living. They are: knowing we can choose our own values, choosing what is important to us, and adopting moral values and an ethical way of life.

Now, let's reconsider this foundation in another way.

These three essential elements are interrelated. By this I mean: We can choose our own values *only* when we realize that we can do so, and we can live ethically *only* after we have embraced ethical values.

Moreover, the values we choose ultimately shape us. For as we live with them, they affect how we act and how we perceive our world. So our choice of a moral way of life influences our ideas, our specfic actions, and who we become.

How we see things and how we act are intertwined. Each makes its mark on the other. When we act on our own choices, we are able to enjoy new experiences and develop alternative ways of behaving. In response, our perceptions may be altered. If this occurs, our new way of seeing the world can change our attitudes. These new sensibilities and attitudes then provide a framework for living. In short, there is a reciprocal relationship here: our perceptions can affect what we are predisposed to do—just as our actions can influence how we see things.[20]

Let's look at what can happen to us when we adopt two facets of ethical living—knowing we can choose our own values and choosing them.

When we realize that we can choose our own values, we see ourselves as a shaper of our own lives. We have power. Once we understand ourselves in this way, we're likely to focus on what we have and what we can do. We are inclined to explore our capabilities and the world. We are likely to conceive of new possibilities for ourselves. There is a place for hope.

Upon knowing we can choose our own values, we could select the ones we want and try to live by them. Then we would experience ourselves as a source of action and change. For we can sense our energies in the present and know that they can direct our future. Thus, we're likely to find value in ourselves and experience security from within. Moreover, it becomes easier to have positive attitudes and feelings toward life because we know we can mold ourselves and our way of living.

Much more can be said about this approach to life. Let's discuss some other ramifications.

Those who determine what is and what is not important to them are on the road to making sense of their own lives. They are less likely to become overwhelmed by available options. They have a way to sort things out: priorities can be established. And these individuals can give the world meaning and significance.

Moreover, as we invest reality with our own values, a transformation takes place. We become more connected and committed to our lives. Our experiences acquire meaning and become significant. We are likely to engage in our lives with greater enthusiasm. We're energized. On the other hand, if we do not give life our own meaning, we may be able to describe what we do, but there is no *felt* import. There's an emptiness instead. Life is flat.[21]

As we better understand our own values, we become more sensitive to their comparative worth. Thus, we not only possess elements critical for making decisions, but we also have a foundation for coping with options. Moreover, as our comprehension develops, we are likely to experience a greater sense of calm and a feeling that life is more manageable.

When we accept what we can do, project realistic goals and achieve them much of the time, we are in a position to feel content. We understand what we are doing. We've chosen to do it. And we have a sense of command over ourselves and our actions. When we thus become aware of our own freedom, stress is reduced.[22] Moreover, by knowing what matters and living as if it does, we possess a necessary ingredient for being happy.

Making Decisions

Decision-making entails reflecting on the situation we're in, assessing it for ourselves, and determining the best thing to do.

Initially, it is not easy. The process of making choices can be fraught with uncertainty, heavily laden with responsibility, and sometimes downright tedious. Choosing among alternatives in new situations always presents a challenge. In time, however, our feelings of uncertainty are more tolerable. Thinking through our possibilities is less difficult. Patience with the process itself develops. And so it begins to feel easier. Finally, this becomes the way we live; it's integral to our lives.

Unfortunately, there are horrific times in life, when there are *no* satisfying options. Circumstances are so terrible that, even though we make the best choices we can, we are unable to feel happy. Nevertheless, by knowing we arrived at the best possible decision, we can still feel centered and retain a sense of command over ourselves. Such awareness will promote a feeling of security, although the overall situation may not engender happiness.[23]

Certainly, this second aspect of living ethically—choosing our own values—is not easy to do. Risks are involved. For the choices we make never guarantee us "a bed of roses." But living morally is, I maintain, still the best alternative. With the others—we risk losing our selves.

Now let's look at several ways to avoid making choices.

Living Without A Self: Just a Hole

Some people do not take time to discover their options and to consider the relative desirability of each. This means they do not have a framework of values for determining their own actions. As a consequence, they cannot figure out what they want to do; for without goals, they are left aimless.

Once circumstances become pressing and unpleasant, such people are apt to flail about. They are *out of control*. Now control is certainly not *the* goal in life. But rudderless people feel awry, trying to navigate through these situations with no constructive means of steering themselves.

There can be a number of reasons for this. Perhaps they cannot sort out the predicaments they're in because they do not have the patience. Or they may not have the ability to think through available alternatives. Or they may have no values and convictions which can serve as a foundation for action. Other factors could also render them unable to devise a satisfying strategy for guiding their choices. So they remain adrift.

A number of repercussions can follow from living without having our own values. For instance, when we're operating in such a state, we do not have a secure self to relate to. So we're likely to experience loneliness. Feeling lonely may not even be apparent to the person who is experiencing it, as loneliness can be camouflaged by a steady stream of distractions. Different things can fill the bill—work, hobbies or, ironically enough, having people around all the time. And when none of these diversions are available, the television or radio will do. In spite of efforts to relieve it, the feeling of isolation prevails.

Some who lack an internal self never adopt any values for themselves. Instead, to get by, they pattern their behavior on the actions of others. The source copied can be, for example, someone from the media, a leading authority, a person from an organization, or a group; it can even be a friend or spouse. In each instance, these individuals, devoid of any values of their own, simply mimic someone else.

When the model loses its power or the distraction wanes, these people are left to their own inner resources. There they find either nothing—or chaos.

The task then becomes: How can I fill the void within? Or—how can I hide from it? Or—how can I quiet down the chaos?

Loneliness is ready to set in. Insomnia may very well follow. Compulsive behavior—eating, shopping, drinking, following routines, working, talking, etc.—is an easy out. The frustration of living this way, without a clue as to how to change it, may even lead to violence.

Often "uppers" or "downers" are taken to override the feelings of emptiness. Sleeping pills, narcotics, drugs and alcohol—all provide a way to get by without looking at what's going on within.

The effects of these contrivances are short-lived, for the condition within one's self has not been addressed. When the efficacy of the mind-altering vehicle wears off, the users revert to their original state. Feelings of nothingness and/or chaos return. The choice then becomes enduring these painful feelings or resorting again to a stop-gap mechanism to shut it down temporarily. The cycle is unending. Those who continue in this way remain victims of themselves—prey to their own internal state. They feel cornered and powerless to do anything about it.

There's a sharp contrast between the dominant feelings in these two modes of living. In one we experience a sense of our own self; and we feel centered, empowered, capable and free. In the other we experience a lack of self-possession; and we feel helpless—and trapped. Whichever orientation to life we choose not only affects our feelings but also can influence how we appear to others—a factor which may impact on our relationships and our professional lives.

- *Do you know people who seem either to be centered or to lack self-possession?*
- *How does their approach to living appear to affect their lives?*

The points made here about using your own values to shape your life hold true for *all* value choices, including moral ones.

We have just considered the benefits of living by our own values. Now let's ask ourselves: Why should we select *ethical* values instead of some other kind? Why should we be moral?

Let's go on to explore this.

Chapter VIII

ഇഠരു

Why Be Moral?

Different Strokes for Different Folks

Why be moral? There are many ways to answer this question. Some people respond in a flash. "You should." Why? "Because it's better." When pressed still further, they respond, "It's better because it just is!"

To them being moral is definitely the best way to act. It's obvious. They offer no reasons and require none. They simply say, "It's the right way to live." Others defend their way of life with a phrase such as: "It's God's command," or "That's the way I was raised," or "My pastor says it's right."

Many of these individuals identify morality with their own customs and the specific choices they have made. Their mode of life is the only acceptable one. When they encounter different practices, they're quick to say, "That's wrong!"[24]

All sorts of activities are subjected to this judgment. Let's look at a couple of them.

Beth has a caring, supportive relationship with her boyfriend Ken, but she chooses not to live with him. If anyone lives with a girlfriend or boyfriend, Beth does not approve. She just thinks it's always wrong to live together unless you are married. My friend Felipe approaches church-going in the same way. Felipe thinks that everyone should go to religious services weekly. He does. This is his top priority. Not attending church every week is simply unacceptable.

Others agree we ought to base our lives on moral values. But in contrast to Beth and Felipe, these people believe certain activities are not good or bad in themselves. For them each action is rendered unique by the time, place and conditions in which it occurs. Therefore its moral worth can determined *only* within its own individual context.

They maintain that we act morally only if we select our actions so as to create the most favorable consequences for people. When we succeed, the specific action chosen is the *right* one. The moral worth of each particular action is derived from its effects. So before acting, they consider the possible consequences of an action. They ask such questions as: "What repercussions will there be?" "Will anyone be harmed?" "Will anyone be helped?" "Is this the best I can do for them?"

Just as people and situations differ, so do the kinds of actions that may fulfill these requirements and could, as a result, be designated "right." But for these individuals there is only one way to be moral. It is: to want to do what is right and to do it. They believe that moral values—respecting and valuing people—should govern our actions. And that it's good to bring moral values into the world; whereas being harmful or indifferent to others is not.

In contrast to this ethical group, there's another segment of the population who wonder if they ought to be moral at all. They are aware of immorality around them. They hear that only fools don't break the rules. They accept the pressure to be "open-minded" and believe that "anything is O.K." Having no bond with an ethical code, they think it makes no difference whether anyone chooses or doesn't choose to be moral; ethical actions have no special importance—all ways of life are of equal value. So for them, the phrase "different strokes for different folks" applies to all ways of life. Are they correct?

Why should anyone live morally?

Is ethical action worth doing?

Or is it good only because it's a way of avoiding punishment by God or the law?

Let's approach these questions pragmatically. By this I mean: Let's see what might happen when we embrace ethical values and live accordingly.[25]

How can we be affected by living in this way?
What kind of people are we likely to become?
What kind of life will we probably lead?
What kind of a world could we help to create?

Affirm—Extend—Connect

As we proceed, let's keep this thought in mind: Once we make the decision to be moral, living ethically has two facets—adopting ethical ideals and employing them for ethical action.

Previously we saw that regardless of what our values are, whenever we embrace values and live with them as our guide, they'll be reflected in our actions. The longer we live this way, the more we become our own person and bring the meaning we want into our lives. Thus, we mold ourselves and our environment.

O.K., but—What specifically happens to us when we adopt our own values and principles and some of these are in fact ethical?

One result is that while we are abiding by ethical values, our ability to relate to others improves. Several factors contribute to this: As moral individuals, we *appreciate personal uniqueness*, an approach whereby everyone is respected for who he or she is. We readily *listen* to others, and they are *heard*. And we *respond* to them in view of who they are, not just in terms of how they can fit into our plans. Whenever the person with whom we are interacting also is a moral agent, the communication is mutual.

So as we live with moral values, the scope of our concern includes not only our own well-being but the welfare of others as well. We affirm the importance of all people, treating them as worthwhile simply because of their humanity.

To take on a moral way of life is obviously our own decision. When we put it into practice, we do not abandon ourselves. To the contrary: we just perceive others, like ourselves, as worthy of respect.

When we respect ourselves, it's easier to appreciate others. Moreover, when we express a positive attitude toward them, we also affirm life and ourselves. As a result, our sense of self-worth increases.

This is a self-perpetuating cycle. Self-affirmation lays the groundwork for being positive toward others. Affirming others builds our self-respect, which, in turn, increases our capacity to reach out to others. So, by all accounts, our personal welfare is clearly linked to the well-being of others.

This implies, at the very least, that when we're ethical, we don't abuse ourselves or others. And whenever possible, we avoid hurting people and try to protect them from harm. When we're moral, *every* method of undermining others is wrong. Therefore, *any* form of manipulation is unacceptable. We do not treat people as objects—even for our noblest ends. Being moral is a nonviolent approach to living. It is life-affirming: the very antithesis of destructiveness.

Individuals who live morally are not interested in having power over others. They refrain from a variety of activities, including: lying to others; dismissing them; arguing them down; manipulating them through flattery; intimidating them; and physically coercing them.

As a "Yes!" to life, living morally means living expansively with respect to people. All are worthy of care. There's a desire which propels us to help others and to be good to our own self.

When we care about other people as well as ourselves, we try our best to recognize the special qualities of each one. As we take into consideration the diversity of individual concerns, desires and needs, we do not react to all of them in the same fashion or merely parrot learned responses. Consequently, we find the prevalent prejudices toward children, minorities, women or the current underdog unacceptable. We try to be impartial—to treat each person equally well. Others might then refer to us and our conduct as "just." They're apt use the term "just" to describe those actions which are directed toward a group of people with the express purpose of treating each of those individuals equally well.

If we do use the word "just" to refer to our own acts, we're most likely to do so when their intent is to positively affect a group of people to whom we are not close. In contrast, we are less inclined to consider our acts as "just" when they involve those with whom we are intimate. We're simply not prone to think we should try to treat them justly. Instead, we're usually predisposed to act caringly toward them. Because of our relationship to each, we're not apt to make a decision to be just. Rather, our affiliation with them usually prompts us to act on their behalf.[26]

- *How have you felt when you've extended yourself to others?*
- *What was it like when you did so for someone with whom you already had a caring relationship?*
- *Was it different when you helped a stranger or an acquaintance?*
- *Do you know people who refrain from acting on behalf of others?*

Becoming More Than I Am

Being ethical means we're not interested in just getting by. Managing to get through the day and augmenting our material and financial assets are not our only concerns. Of course, such preoccupations are necessary for survival; but we strive for more.

When we live morally, we have a positive effect on our associates. We are steadfast in our principles—we're reliable and dependable. The intent of our behavior is predictable. We can be trusted to be as kind as our perceptions and our resourcefulness permit. Others feel safe in our presence. We feel secure with ourselves.

The point to be made here is a simple one. Just as we have an impact on other people, those we're with also affect us. So when we live among destructive, negative people, we expend a good deal of energy buffering their input. In their presence it is much more difficult to use our personal resources for constructive ends than it would be if we were surrounded instead by moral people.

Moral individuals radiate positive energy and recognize us as worthy of respect. They do their best to give us the space we need. They try to keep their promises. Moreover, they can be concerned for us and may even extend themselves to us. Their very presence reinforces our positive attitudes—toward them, ourselves and life. Consequently, we have more energy.[27]

- *Have you ever felt tired after spending time with someone, although beforehand you did not think you were doing anything exhausting?*
- *Have you ever felt more energetic after you've had a conversation?*
- *Why do you think this happened?*

Living with ethical people is likely to have marked effects on us. We're apt to feel peaceful and secure from the consideration shown and from the dependablilty and non-harmful behavior witnessed. A sense of personal freedom is likely to ensue from the power entrusted in us and from the absence of manipulation and control from without.

Moral people can be friends: in their presence personal growth is nourished.

Let's look into what this might mean.

The Good We Reap

What is it like to live in a community of ethical people?

Having no need to defend and protect themselves from their associates, its members feel secure and empowered. They can readily engage in life as it is felt and live in the present rather than focusing only on the future or the past. Their experiences are rich.

Let's consider the quality of these experiences.

Awareness of the present permits moral people to appreciate themselves, their experiences and others. By staying in touch with their world, they feel more alive than those who are not so connected. Relationships are prized for the satisfactions derived from them. They matter.

As moral people begin to feel more secure about life and more positive about themselves, they can find it easier to be hopeful and confident. These attitudes are likely to engender openness and a readiness to immerse oneself in life.

When moral people live in an ethical community, they experience a vital connection to others. They also develop an ability to experience life from various points of view. This capacity entails an increased recognition of each person. When greater understanding ensues, the richness of life unfolds. And living becomes more interesting.[28]

Before we go on, let's sum up what's just been said. We've noticed that being moral engages us more completely in living; it affects the way we feel, what we do, and how we understand our world.

Moral life also brings about a reduction in stress. For stress is determined less by what happens to us than by how we handle it. Our actions, attitudes, and responses make all the difference. Since moral people know that they can determine their own acts, they experience less stress than those who feel powerless.[29]

Moreover, when we willingly extend ourselves to others for their benefit, we can experience a calm within us comparable to the states often achieved by running, yoga, and meditation. As we reach these inner conditions, we not only feel better, but we're actually doing something that's good for our health. We get a high. We experience increased energy and less emotional stress. This usually means our sense of self-worth and empowerment is increased.

Herbert Benson, a noted Harvard cardiologist who has done work on the "relaxation response," maintains that these kinds of reactions result from a release of endorphins, pain-reducing chemicals which function as our body's natural opiates. When they take effect, our body shifts into a deep state of rest whereby its metabolic rate and blood pressure are decreased.[30]

Living ethically is one way to realize this state.

- *How do you feel when you've done something good for someone else?*

The positive, life-affirming state of mind we achieve while living morally is also beneficial to our bodies.

The experiences of author Norman Cousins demonstrate this phenomenon in a dramatic way. He suffered from ankylosing spondylitis (an often fatal disease), and was told that medical science had done all it could. Norman Cousins decided to try one more tact—to withdraw from everyday life and bombard himself with humor. For days he engulfed himself in laughter as he watched Marx Brothers movies. After that, his illness went into remission.[31]

In a similar vein, others have realized that mental imagery can help arrest the course of an illness: it is known to have sent cancer and other progressively destructive diseases into remission. There has been a growing trend among holistic health practitioners to harness this power.

Moreover, living within a network of supportive people (such as a group of moral friends) has proven to be a stress reducer.[32] Ethical individuals do sustain one another, whereas people living a competitive life style do not have this support and are more vulnerable to stress.

Our feelings can be a key to understanding the nature of our relationships. Once we know the feelings that arise in response to one kind of social situation, we can better recognize the nature of a new interpersonal environment by noticing the feelings it engenders and comparing them to others.

- *How do you feel after you've been with someone who embodies a positive approach to life?*
- *How did you feel after you could no longer be with someone who cared about you?*
- *How do you feel when you are with moral people? with competitive ones?*

The Good We Create

When we're in a moral relationship, giving is reciprocated. Bonds are formed. The sense of cohesion we experience transforms each of us.

As a person acts morally, he or she sets an example and creates a pattern of living for others to see. By their very actions, ethical people encourage others to be moral. Thus the community of ethical persons to which we belong is likely to expand. And the milieu in which we can comfortably live a moral life is apt to broaden. So there's a greater chance we'll be treated ethically.

Because we all affect each other, anything we do has a ripple effect. For example, let's consider a relationship you could have with someone (whom, for purposes of illustration, we'll call John). If you act in morally good ways toward John, he is more likely to be considerate of his neighbor Jane. Jane is now apt to be kinder to Sue, and so forth. People who are aware of this sort of chain reaction sometimes say: "What goes around comes around."

My point here is that by living morally, we not only benefit ourselves by our actions, but we simultaneously make an impact on our community. And we affect the conditions in which we live.

To clarify what's been said here, we'll now look at those people who do not live morally and who also do not live with people who are moral.

What's likely to happen to them?

Things We Avoid

When we are immoral and do not live among ethical individuals, we are likely to get caught up in the competition so prevalent in modern society.

Let's look once again at this situation, but this time let's do so from another perspective.

In a competitive context, life is evaluated on a win-lose basis. So if you win, I lose. And if I win, you lose. The goal is superiority and power over others. This is considered—success! "Winner" status depends upon others being less, doing less, or having less. One must at all cost avoid being a loser. When you can't achieve more than you already have or outshine another, you can always devalue someone else. Then you can think you're a winner.

If you adopt this mode, you will be aggressive toward everyone who might impede you: they are obstacles in your path, adversaries to be overcome.

O.K. So let's suppose you win. It looks good. But much more has occurred: you've lost, too.

For when victory in a win-lose world determines your own value, life feels precarious. Self-worth can be demolished in an instant. It rides on winning. The stakes are high. The game is played hard. Life feels hard.

When all are competitors, everyone is "looking out for #1." So no one can be trusted. There can be no mutual support. For survival's sake, everybody is defensive. Life is approached as if violence were a constant threat.

Keeping to oneself and/or self-insulation, however, can reduce the likelihood of harm. But when we live without mutual trust or support, friendship is not possible.

- *Have you ever been in a crisis with no supportive person around? How does it compare to the times when friends were there for you?*

Competitiveness, expressed as the desire to have power over others, is found in all forms of enslavement and domination. It can be manifested by treating someone unfairly—for example, when he or she is not given "due process" in a court of law.

Sometimes the desire to exert power over others appears in a very "civilized" guise and is rarely noticed. It often takes the form of mind games.

Occasionally the people playing these mind games give the impression of being kind: They just seem to "feel sorry" for the other person and are merely trying to "help." These subtle put-downs assume various forms and arise in diverse situations. For example, Jack explained a map to Alice, thinking that she could not decipher it on her own. Vivian acted as if Charles could not make arrangements for his own vacation and did it for him. Without being asked for advice, George told Eric which school to attend. Sarah tried to convince her sister that the trip she had planned would be too arduous for her. All these actions can be confused with helpfulness, but at times they have another intent—to belittle the person. The difference can often be felt.

This game may also be conducted through flattery. Upon close scrutiny, the real purpose becomes apparent: it is to define the other person in a limiting fashion.

The interchange between Jim and Bob is a case in point. My friend Jim was encouraged by Bob to become a lab technician. Bob told Jim that he would make a fine technician because he had an ability to be careful with detail, worked well with sophisticated machinery, and wanted to promote people's health. This was all true. Bob surely recognized some of Jim's talents and interests. But he did not take into account other things he knew about Jim. He failed to acknowledge Jim's gift for relating to others, his keen intelligence, his immense drive, his ability to remember vast amounts of information, and his talent for using both intuition and analysis to assess situations. With all these aptitudes going for him, Jim had the potential to be competent in any number of other professions as well. He could realistically set his sights on becoming a physician, a physical therapist or a psychiatrist, to mention only a few. By excluding these options, Bob's discussion projected a limited future for Jim.

- *Do you know someone who acts in these ways?*
- *What other mind games have you noticed?*
- *What are they like?*

Sometimes a competitive tack on life is revealed as envy. Envious people deal with life from a win-lose perspective, comparing themselves to other people and taking note of what others have and do. If "the envious" also like what these individuals own and admire the events in their lives, they want the same—but exclusively for themselves.

Envy is destructive to the persons envied. Negative forces stream forth from "the envious" as they pit themselves against others. This energy can be actively blocked out and interpreted as invalid by the envied; or it can be felt and absorbed as a negative blow. In both cases the recipients' energy is dissipated—either by fending off the envy expressed or by being worn down in its presence.

But envy is not only destructive to its targets; it also impairs those consumed by envy. These people define themselves through the lives of others. Their goals and desires arise to mirror other people. They have no personal center with values. As the aspirations of individuals around them change, so do their own. Therefore, their envy continually throws them off balance and consumes their energy. So vitality for other things is diminished. To be sure, those who are obsessed by envy turn themselves into victims.

The point here is that envy erodes the envious person's capacity to be moral. And it is detrimental to everyone involved.

- *Have you ever been envious?*
- *How did it feel?*
- *What do you think it would be like to go through life feeling envious?*

Lying can also be found in a competitive life.

It is commonly defined as communicating something you know is not true under the pretense that it is. It includes verbal and nonverbal messages. Since, on face value, it seems to be a gestural or verbal act, lying is not customarily viewed as a vehicle for competition, coercion, violence or human destruction. Well—it can be. Here's why.

With a lie, we know there's a deliberate attempt to misinform.

But what else happens?

When a lie is believed, it has the power to influence someone's thoughts, feelings and actions. Then it functions as a method of control that could erode the foundation upon which the believer acts. When a lie succeeds in determining beliefs, it can influence actions.

A lie very often causes even more harm than overt violence does. When we believe a lie, our power to deal with the world is undermined. The basis for our actions—knowledge—is destroyed.

But sometimes a lie is told to protect someone else or even ourselves. As we noted in chapter III, we might do more harm by telling our ill friend how weak she looks than by not being truthful. And in potentially violent situations, it might be better to lie than to reveal what we know. In both instances, the hurt to be avoided seems to be greater than the damage caused by the lie.

If, however, a lie is discovered, other unfortunate things occur. The person upon whom the lie was perpetrated may feel betrayed and could become less trusting of people. He or she could also feel resentment toward the liar and might even begin to doubt the veracity of everyone. A lie can have these adverse effects only because its recipient believed the liar was telling the truth. This fact gives the lie its power. Once the truth has been discovered, the lie loses its strength, but the person who believed it may feel set off balance, disappointed or angry.

- *Have you ever discovered a lie?*
- *What effect did this have on you?*

When a liar succeeds in misleading people, the lie may protect him or her by impressing or subduing others. Misrepresenting the truth may then seem like a clever move.

But by lying, the liar has broken the tacit promise we all make when we communicate with each other—the promise to tell the truth.

Liars strive to keep the lie intact. To do so, they may create a separation between themselves and the persons to whom they have lied. A chasm remains until the lie is revealed. As a consequence, liars don't feel close to those whom they have duped.

Is lying worth it?

Chronic liars often think it is. They're likely to feel that the immediate edge to be secured is most important. This need governs their lies. But, ironically, people who lie jeopardize not only their integrity but their personal power as well. For every time a lie is discovered, the liar's words carry less and less weight. Trust in the liar is slowly eroded. Known liars are not readily believed. And over time, their capacity to influence others dwindles; eventually they may no longer be viewed as trustworthy.

But even if lies are not discovered, they are damaging to the liar. For lies can wreak havoc on the connections liars experience—both to themselves and to their surroundings. As they lie, fibbers may override and discount their own memories. For those who lie habitually, it can become increasingly difficult to determine what is real. Their sense of self is slowly worn away. The moorings for their life become loose. Two major sources of security—knowledge and a sense of reality—are gone.

A group of lifelong liars who know that everyone else in their midst is also a liar can never create a community. Nor can they, as disconnected people, experience a sense of belonging. And since they can't believe anyone in the group, they have no basis for relating or communicating. They remain just an aggregate of separate individuals.[33]

- *Do you know people who make a habit of lying?*
- *What long-term effects has it had on you? on them? on others?*
- *What advantages have they gained?*
- *Do you think it is worth it?*

Just like the act of lying, cheating on a partner breaks up the solidarity and connectedness in a relationship. Yet when the couple is married, sexual infidelity is often referred to as an "extramarital affair," as if it were an activity of no more consequence than any other. Today unfaithfulness is commonplace among public figures and has become a way of life for many others. It's an adventure! It breaks up the monotony of living. It seems to make some people feel good.

But—what else does it do?

As I see it, infidelity not only breaks promises but also damages integrity. Here's why.

If we want to sustain a relationship with the person to whom we've been unfaithful, we often cover up what we have done. These compensatory actions create the impression that our commitment has not been broken. But, in fact, living in this mode is similar to being with someone to whom we have lied. And it brings with it all the repercussions that we've seen arise when we cover up a lie—and possibly more!

The bond between the people involved is damaged. For cheaters treat their partners merely as objects—pawns that merit no respect. Yet some believe that occasionally extramarital affairs have a positive value. For instance, sometimes they shore up the unfaithful so that they can be more effective parents or perhaps more adequately care for an ill spouse. In such cases, cheating on a partner may seem to be worth doing.

But a risk nevertheless is taken. Like lying, if the infidelity is discovered, faith and trust in the cheater are eroded. A price is paid.

Yet at times both lying and infidelity seem to inflict less harm on the people affected by them than any other alternative. In such circumstances, those who believe an action's value is determined by its effects view these choices as the least undesirable ones.

- *What does the acceptance of extramarital affairs tell you about our expectations for partnered relationships?*
- *Do you know any people who have had an affair?*
- *What effects did it have on them? their spouse or partner? their children? their relationships?*

To sum up, infidelity and lying are not moral acts. In time, they damage not only the people who engage in them and the persons whose lives they touch directly, but also the communities in which they all live. To me, the human destructiveness wrought by infidelity and lying—as well as by the win-lose mentality, mind games, and envy—places these practices on a continuum with murder. The likelihood of becoming subjected to them is greatly reduced, however, if we live morally among ethical individuals.

Let us move on.

Throughout history people have been aware of the effects of ethical and unethical behavior on individuals and on the societies in which they live. A vast body of literature—both fiction and nonfiction, in the humanities and in the social sciences—has investigated this subject. Thus far we have only looked at moral behavior, or the lack thereof, in the lives of individuals.

If we were to consider ethics from the viewpoint of society at large, we would get a glimpse of the range of its effects on the social complex. Then we could begin to appreciate how moral living impacts on a society, helps to shape its character and, in turn, influences the lives of its members.

The next chapter explores ethics from this broader perspective.

Chapter IX

Ethics and Society

Historical Roots

The guidelines for ethical living found in Western culture today are based largely on the Hebrew Scriptures and the writings of the ancient Greek philosophers. These sources have provided the two primary orientations for Western ethics—namely, prohibitions for deterring people from harming each other and ideals for human development. Over the centuries such standards have been assimilated with Christian values and modified in a variety of ways, but these core ideas still remain the foundation for ethics in the West.

The two societies within which these ideas arose differed greatly, as did the lives of their respective populations. So it comes as no surprise to see ethics and values playing dissimilar roles in each of them.

The ancient Hebrews were without a secure, permanent home. Cohesion and stability could not be derived from the physical conditions of their lives; these qualities were derived instead from commonly held precepts for living. Such codes of behavior were transmitted orally from one generation to the next for several hundred years. They were then written down and eventually became a part of what we know as the Old Testament of the Bible, or the Hebrew Scriptures.

Through commandments the Hebrews set forth standards for right and wrong actions. The primary goal was to regulate how people treated each other. In addition, these moral guidelines provided the Hebrews with a commonly held set of beliefs for relating to each other. All who adopted this code of behavior had the same internalized principles for acting. Orderly relationships were made possible. In an uncertain world, morality served as a stabilizer for each individual and as a source of cohesion for this community.

Today moral beliefs can still serve us in these ways. Modern societies also welcome cohesion and stability. When we find ourselves in a new locale, our own integrated set of beliefs provides us with a familiar source of structure and a sense of continuity. And when we've lived in one place for a long time, moral principles can reinforce the security we often feel from having a permanent home.

The commands in the Hebrew Scriptures involve many aspects of human behavior. Yet, although some are concerned with how we should think of others, most tell us what we should *not* do to them. They are primarily prohibitions—we should not allow our impulses to run wild. Rather, we should keep them in check and restrain ourselves from inflicting harm on others.

Exodus is one of the books in the Hebrew Scriptures. There we find the Ten Commandments enumerated. We are told that God gave these divine instructions to Moses on Mount Sinai. Here are some of the moral dictums found in chapter 20 of Exodus:

> Honour your father and your mother, that you may have a long life in the land which the Lord, your God, is giving you.
>
> You shall not kill.
>
> You shall not commit adultery.
>
> You shall not steal.
>
> You shall not bear false witness against your neighbour.
>
> You shall not covet your neighbour's house. You shall not covet your neighbour's wife, nor his male or female slave, nor his ox or ass, nor anything else that belongs to him."[34]

Six hundred years later the moral teachings in the book of Exodus were expanded. The new section is called Leviticus, chapter 19. There it is written:

You shall not steal. You shall not lie or speak falsely to one another. . . .

You shall not defraud or rob your neighbour. You shall not withhold overnight the wages of your day laborer. You shall not curse the deaf, or put a stumbling block in front of the blind, but you shall fear your God. I am the LORD.

You shall not act dishonestly in rendering judgment. Show neither partiality to the weak nor deference to the mighty, but judge your fellow men justly. You shall not go about spreading slander among your kinsmen; nor shall you stand by idly when your neighbor's life is at stake. I am the LORD.

You shall not bear hatred for your brother in your heart. Though you may have to reprove your fellow man, do not incur sin because of him. Take no revenge and cherish no grudge against your fellow countrymen. You shall love your neighbor as yourself. I am the LORD. . . .

When an alien resides with you in your land, do not molest him. You shall treat the alien who resides with you no differently than the natives born among you; have the same love for him as for yourself; for you too were once aliens in the land of Egypt. I, the LORD, am your God, who brought you out of the land of Egypt. Be careful then, to observe all my statutes and decrees. I am the LORD."[35]

People generally do not express themselves with this kind of language today, but these goals are still upheld by moral people in the West.

The Bible lends itself to a number of interpretations. As it is written, references to "the Lord" and to "the Lord our God" emphasize that these commands came from God. Their authority originates from God. Obedience is required because these are God's wishes.

Some people today recognize God as the source of these teachings and the ground for their validity. Others do not: they may embrace such guidelines simply because no better ones seem to exist. They do not believe in God and therefore have no reason to follow commands that are said to have come from God. Other individuals who adopt this code believe in God but think that the Hebrew Scriptures do not contain the words of God. Nevertheless, both groups try to live according to the commands found in these scriptures because doing so has a positive effect on their lives. Their decision is a practical one based on their own judgment.

Christianity gave the moral teachings in the Hebrew Scriptures a new life. Emphasis was then placed on being charitable to all and caring for others, even strangers and enemies. Christian beliefs are written in the New Testament of the Bible.

Islam is another religion in the Judaeo-Christian tradition. The Koran, revered as the primary work of Muslim scripture, contains many of the moral commands found within the Old and New Testaments: There are, for example, prohibitions against lying, stealing, adultery and murder; and the virtues of honesty, kindness, courage and generosity (among others) are extolled.

Judaism, Christianity, and Islam each strongly influenced the development of ethics in Western culture. These three monotheistic religions not only established rules for how people should live with one another but also were instrumental in conveying these values to successive generations.

- *Do you think there are good reasons for obeying the guides for living just discussed? If you answer "yes," then ask yourself: Which of these moral laws do I accept? Why?*
- *Do you know people who disregard any of them? What effects do these people have on you? What effects do they seem to have on others?*

The ancient Greek philosophers also strongly influenced Western culture's way of thinking about ethical behavior.

Most of these wise men lived in Athens, a prosperous city-state located on the Aegean Sea. There they found security in a permanent home and a booming economy. With their daily needs met, survival was not an issue. The early Greek philosophers had leisure time to inquire into all aspects of life. Merely living was not enough for them. They wanted to know how to live well. Having a deep appreciation for human beings, they cast their eyes beyond everyday matters to find ideals for human development and life.

The two foremost philosophers of ancient Greece—Plato and Aristotle—left us a vast legacy of ideas about values and the best ways to live.

Their approach is quite different from that of the ancient Hebrews. In contrast, the ancient Greeks do not primarily exhort us to avoid doing certain things. And they do not command us to treat ourselves and others in a particular way. Instead, to promote an understanding of what constitutes a good life, their works explore various ways of living. Examples of good ways to live are provided, and the essential features of a good person are delineated. These philosophical works profess that a good society is possible if there are good people, and that such a society will, in turn, foster good people.[36]

From these two philosophers we've received most of our ideas about virtues, or in other words, admirable ways of conducting ourselves. The ideals they named include prudence, temperance, courage, wisdom, justice, liberality, magnificence, piety, friendliness and loyalty.

People throughout the history of Western civilization have refined the meaning and significance of these Greek ideals. Some have cited other human traits as also highly desirable: The Christian ideal of charity is a case in point. But the mainstay of ethical ideals for Western culture was created by the ancient Greeks.

- *Are any of these virtues more important to you than others?*
- *Does one of these traits seem to appear most frequently in the people you know? If so, why?*
- *In your experience, are some of the virtues found primarily among the members of one sex or one age group?*
- *Do you discount any of these virtues? Why?*
- *Do you consider other characteristics virtuous?*

Today we're not inclined to speak of virtues. Instead, we're more likely to recognize the importance of role models for the young and to be aware of our own desire for admirable persons to emulate. The words have changed, but the goals remain the same. Nowadays we seek exemplary figures who also embody the prohibitions in the Old Testament and embody some of the ideals found in the writings of ancient religious and philosophical thinkers.

We want the younger generation to copy good examples. Schools often provide students with fine role models. These admirable individuals may be located in the academic community itself, or they may be great leaders in history or fictional heroes. Such human beings express a wealth of desirable character traits and thereby open up possibilities for us all. As exemplary figures, they indirectly provide guidance. And when we keep them in mind, we can more easily focus our energies on higher goals.

- *Whom have you admired?*
- *What effect did this have on you?*
- *Have you ever been with someone you couldn't respect?*
- *Did this affect you? How?*

Down through the centuries many people have thought we should learn to live by ethical commands and ideals. Those who succeed in this endeavor would transcend their pre-socialized nature and become what human beings ought to be: "civilized."

For sure, ethical behavior can be viewed as a civilizing force. We may not feel comfortable thinking of ourselves as needing to become "civilized," or more fully human. But we do not have *inborn* patterns of action with which to live morally; instead, human beings themselves *create* ethical ideals which they can elect to emulate. Following moral precepts and striving for ethical ideals are important as we develop a moral life. In trying to live according to such ideals, we seek out certain tendencies, attitudes and actions. Others are curbed. Thus we evolve.

My point here has been that individuals in Western civilization have formulated moral precepts, ethical ideals, and notions of what constitutes a good life—tools with which they hoped to shape people's lives. Their goal has been two-pronged: to develop virtuous people who live well and to create a good society.

To this end, civilizations have created a variety of practices, customs and laws designed to implement moral ideals by deterring unethical behavior.

Let's look at a few currently in practice.

Rules, Laws, and Formalities

Many things are taught to us when we're young. Often an adult just says to a child, "You should do it." Or "You should say it." No explanation is offered. These directives frequently seem like mere social formalities or rules of politeness; yet they may very well be efforts to instill certain attitudes fundamental to being moral.

Let's look at two common vehicles of politeness: "please" and "thank you." Like many youngsters, I was told as a child that whenever I ask for something, I should say "please." That's polite. I see now that if I also acknowledge the meaning of "please" while saying it, I concurrently recognize the other person as worthy of respect. Then, when I say "please," my approach is gentle and appreciative. It is not aggressive and demanding.

"Thank you," I was told, should be said after someone agrees to do something that we believe is good, and also after such a deed has been done. In both instances saying "thank you" expresses my gratitude.

Of course, "please" and "thank you" may be said mechanically, purely out of habit, with no awareness of the other person involved. But these expressions are meant to convey an attitude essential to being moral— namely, respect for other people. By teaching children to say "please" and "thank you" and by assisting them to understand the reasons behind the words, we can begin to foster a considerate attitude.

Also worthy of attention is how a society fosters social welfare. By their very existence, social welfare programs can promote the belief that people are worthwhile. Some policies for helping others demonstrate the importance of beneficence and provide ways of realizing this moral ideal. A prime example of this sort of policy is a government which offers health care to those who cannot afford their own. All those who participate in its implementation—including the lawmakers who pass the legislation and the taxpayers whose taxes support these measures—can enhance their own moral character by acting on behalf of those in need.

Many civil laws, as well as these humane governmental policies, also promote ethical values.

Laws and judicial procedures express moral values when they protect the rights of the individuals under their jurisdiction and treat all of them equally well. A law which advocates treating people fairly is considered just. Justice is an ideal in democratic countries. In such societies, courts of law are instituted to ensure a fair enforcement of civil laws.

Governments live up to this democratic ideal when they espouse such rights as "Life, Liberty and the pursuit of Happiness" for all their people. Laws endeavor to achieve these goals when they restrain people from infringing on each other's lives. A police force and punishments (e.g., fines and imprisonment) are established to deter people from breaking civil laws. Acts such as theft, assault and murder are considered crimes in a secular context. In our society the laws created to curb these acts—as well as many other civil laws—mirror the religious ones found in the Hebrew Scriptures. But the words for the transgressions differ: In a civil context these acts are considered "illegal"; whereas in the religious one they are called "immoral."

Laws not only accord respect to people who may be harmed by others; they also are meant to protect people from endangering themselves. Traffic laws exemplify this intention. Rules of the road are designed expressly to prevent us from causing accidents.

Stringent limitations are often placed on the young to keep them from harming themselves and others. Setting a legal age for drinking alcoholic beverages and establishing a minimum age for driving an automobile are two cases in point. Some members of society think that prior to a "certain age" people are not mature enough to handle these tasks responsibly.

Laws like these are essentially preventive measures. They are designed to keep people from hurting each other; and they're often successful.

These safeguards do, at the very least, promote decorum. In the best case scenario, however, they can contribute to public safety and security, as well as provide a framework for peaceful living. But let's remember— a fair legal system and just laws cannot create moral individuals. Such structures alone are unable to mold perceptions and motivations. And, obviously, they cannot control people's actions.

- *Do you think special limitations should be placed on minors? If so—What kinds? For whom? Why?*

Moral laws and values also provide the foundation for many school practices.

Numerous examples can be cited. To begin, let's consider teachers who want to be fair: They often reward good behavior and punish those who disobey school policies. Sometimes instructors deliberately forewarn their students of the negative repercussions for undersirable acts, hoping to convince them to act in a law-abiding fashion. By so doing, these teachers are acting in the time-honored traditions of Judaism, Christianity and Islam—traditions which strive to deter people from breaking God's laws by warning them of the possibility of punishment.

School rules, like ideal civil laws, often maintain that each punitive measure should be appropriate for its corresponding infraction. And they also may specify comparable penalties for similar wrongdoings. Any institution which functions in this manner has established "just" procedures.

Many academic institutions also strive to nurture attitudes and personality traits fundamental to moral living. Efforts are made to increase sensitivity to and respect for all people. Literature, history and diverse cultures are studied to develop the students' understanding of people and to increase their ability to empathize with others. School programs try to develop students' knowledge of virtuous individuals; to increase their admiration for such ways of living; and to encourage their desire to emulate them. Moreover, the school activities themselves are often designed to foster habits supportive of a moral way of life—habits like orderliness, a sense of fair play, dependability, courtesy, self-control and truthfulness.

- *In what ways have your school experiences fostered moral living?*
- *In what respects have they been successful or unsuccessful?*

Ideals of justice can be embedded in the regulations governing groups. Often it is not difficult to see that an organization's rules facilitate efficient functioning; but on closer scrutiny, we may also see that these procedures promote impartiality and fairness as well. This dual role is frequently revealed in the practices governing a group's meetings. For instance, I belong to a club in which the members in attendance are allowed to contribute their suggestions; yet, according to the by-laws, no one is permitted to take over the discussion, change the topic under consideration without consent from those present, or silence another unless he or she is speaking disrespectfully to someone.

- *Do you think the practices governing the organization(s) to which you belong support moral values?*
- *Have you ever participated in a group that did not have fair rules or procedures? How did this affect you and other people?*

Moreover, society acknowledges individuals who perform virtuous deeds. People applaud those who courageously take risks to help others. Newspapers extol their heroic acts. Members of the armed forces, the police force, firefighters, and private citizens are praised publicly and often given awards for bravery. In the tradition of the ancient Greek philosophers, courage is still perceived as a virtue and rewarded. Moreover, our society also recognizes individuals for their lifelong service to the needy. And it praises people for their charity and beneficence.

Decorum Is Not Enough

I know I've aready said this, but it's very important. So please let me emphasize once again: Rules, laws, and formalities have limited value. At the *very best*, they promote decorum. When they're enforced, society runs more smoothly; and people are less likely to be harmed by each other. Rules, laws, and social formalities cannot, however, make people moral. Why? Because they only create a fairly safe setting from which certain deterrents to living morally have been removed. They do not necessarily influence the inner self; and if they do, their influence alone cannot shape moral perceptions and motivations.

We know that by practicing courtesy, following social customs, and living among others who do likewise, we can be socially acceptable, stay out of trouble and, with some luck, keep ourselves reasonably safe from harm. But surely there's more than this! A good life should entail something else besides fair play. How do we attain friendship and camaraderie? How can we be joyful? And how can we maintain an appreciation of our selves, others and life? Without a doubt, these facets of a satisfying life will not be realized merely by staying within the law. But such elements can indeed become integral to our lives—if we live ethically with others who are ethical, too.

How can we live morally?

As we've already seen, it can be a challenge. There are many contrasting patterns of life in Western societies. Some provide examples of moral living and establish prohibitions which discourage unethical behavior; others prepare the way for immorality, engender it, and even foster its growth.

Locating a moral community in which to reside may be difficult. Yet it is important to expend the necessary effort to find one: for trying to live morally while participating in an immoral context *always* exacts a heavy toll on us.

How do people sustain themselves amidst unethical and ethical patterns of living?

Let's turn to this question now.

PART FOUR

WHO SHOULD I BE?

Chapter X

℘℧

One Way to Go: Split Self/Damaged Self

For sure, two diverse kinds of values impact on us. On the one hand, we are encouraged to live by moral ideals. Yet we're also influenced by society's more vocal elements to adopt competitive "me-first" and "the-more-I've-got-the-better" attitudes. So it is not surprising to find that some people try to live ethically and others get caught up in unethical life styles. Certain other individuals, however, adopt both options intermittently—acting morally in certain situations and immorally in others. A duality is thereby created in their lives and within themselves.

Using a different lens to gain new insights, let's reconsider what it means to live in a competitive milieu.

When interacting with adversaries, people often create a wall around themselves for protection. Then their vulnerabilities are hidden, their feelings concealed.[37] Such individuals are either in the trenches defending themselves or engaged in an attack. Thus, living competitively is like living in a "state of war": The tactics are defensive or offensive. So people don't give of themselves without asking, "What will happen to me?" or "What will I get?" Frequently there's also an element of fear.

Living in a "state of war" exacts a heavy toll—an inordinate amount of energy is expended merely for survival. When in this mode, we guard our feelings. This is very draining and leaves us with less vitality for life-affirming activities. A protective stance also reduces our capacity to feel and makes it more difficult to become wholeheartedly immersed in life. Our sensitivities are dulled, rendering our experiences shallow. We feel emotionally isolated, which increases our vulnerability and intensifies our level of stress. Living in a "state of war" is, to say the least, trying! In time, it erodes our capacity for experiencing fully and for becoming thoroughly engaged in life.[38]

Some people seek relief from such combat by living morally with their friends and families. For them, there is a sharp division between life in the "outside" world and life with those to whom they are close. Their home is a special place—a safe haven. All other locales are alien and potentially dangerous. They approach the beginning of the school or work week with dread and are relieved when it's over.

- *Have you ever felt that you hated your job or disliked going to school?*
- *If so, ask yourself: Do I dislike the work itself? Or do I abhor the conditions in which it is done?*
- *Do I find learning repugnant? Or do I find the time at school unnerving? combative? demoralizing?*

Let's see how these experiences can develop.

Once children reach school age, they usually spend much more time in the "outside" world than they do in the family nest or with friends. If their schools and neighborhoods are in a "state of war," the habits of living under siege are likely to dominate their personalities. Then the mode of living in a war zone can easily spill over into their entire lives. No place is comfortable and secure. Everything seems alien or threatening.

To cope with these opposite orientations to life, some divide their lives into two parts. They're moral with friends and families, but in all other arenas they're "at war." Their lives are often checkered by successive occurrences of stress and relief. Periods of being receptive and giving are juxtaposed with intervals of acting defensive and combative. By living in two different modes, these individuals are fragmented. There's no consistent internal foundation on which they can rely. There is no stable self.

- *Do you relate to people differently when you are at school? at work? at a picnic with friends? at home with your family?*

- *If there are differences, what are they?*
- *How do you feel about living this way?*

Living "at war" or in peace is not always determined by the setting we're in. For many people the time spent with their family, friends, and colleagues is also an occasion for combat. These individuals have no safe place.

Sometimes the family itself is a "mixed bag." For example, parents can be kind and loving toward their children yet compete with their spouse. They may also cheat in the relationship. Then, if the cheater wards off discovery, defensiveness ensues. A chasm is formed. On the other hand, some parents are loving toward each other but show little concern for their children, even to the point of neglecting them and disregarding their best interests. At times this takes the form of parent-child competition. Perceiving their children as competitors can motivate parents to abandon their nurturing role and inflict harm instead.

Like the homefront, work and school environments can be "war zones"; or they can be supportive and life-affirming; or they can be a "mixed bag." For instance, students can form mutually helpful relationships with a few classmates, while they simultaneously ward off others. Honesty may prevail among students who are friends, but these same people may lie to others and cheat on exams. Likewise, in the workplace some employees are moral in their interactions with fellow workers but occasionally steal from the till.

We could go on and on with examples of people who fragment their own selves "to get by." In the final analysis they are all, however, self-destructive.

- *Do you know people who fragment themselves?*
- *Do you compartmentalize yourself?*
- *What are the advantages of this behavior?*

Alternating between these two modes is acceptable to some. They believe it's the only way to live in modern society. Life is dealt with expediently. To go along with the way things are done and to fit in, such persons put on a facade. Over time, shifting from one way of behaving to the other can become familiar and comfortable.

When we adopt this way of living, damage is done. No sense of self persists throughout time. Nor is there a place within our selves to rest or from which we can gain strength. There is no center. We are not integrated. And we do not feel whole.

Moreover, since most of us spend the majority of our time in the "outside" world, the mode of living we experience there can very easily dominate our lives.

But there's no compelling reason why we must adopt a particular way of life found in the "outside" world—just because its familiar. And there's no reason why we need to endure a split within our lives. *Nothing*— not even current social conditions—can *force* us into either one of these patterns. We can instead adopt ideals of our own choosing to serve as the basis for all our actions.

To embark on this road, however, we need confidence in ourselves. With sufficient self-trust we can live by our own ideals. Then our self-respect and the pleasure we take in our own company are likely to increase. Moreover, loneliness will not be an issue, as we always have a friend at hand, our own self. Over time we're apt to become increasingly comfortable living by principles which we ourselves have chosen. And we may pursue our own ideals, even when there's no outside support. Living with integrity provides an experience of wholeness and inner security.

- *Do you know people who are peaceful and content within themselves and yet fully engaged in life?*
- *What are they like?*

To continue exploring this issue, let's see how we might embody these qualities while living within modern society.

Chapter XI

୫୨୦୪

Changing Ourselves

It's Possible!

S ome of the people I know have been able to make significant changes
in themselves. For over the years they have altered the way they
feel, think and act. Their lives testify to this.

What makes self-change possible?

The human capacity for self-awareness is a critical factor in
transforming our selves. Its existence becomes apparent to us whenever
we reflect on our own selves. While engaged in self-reflection, we can
create a space between our thinking processes and our ideas, as well as
between our self and our actions. This internal activity enables us to be
aware of our own thoughts and actions. Self-awareness permits us to
stay in touch with what we are doing, thinking, and feeling now, and
with what we've done, thought, and felt at other times. By engendering
personal understanding, such awareness can serve us while we make
decisions for self-change. And the distance created through self-reflection
allows us to act upon our own selves.

As we have already noted, each of us has a unique way of thinking,
feeling and acting. Consequently, ideas about and responses to the same

situation are apt to differ. This can come to our attention when we are doing things with others and observe a variety of actions and reactions. So it's not surprising to discover that when people reflect on themselves, each one has a unique perception of his or her own identity and of its future.

- *The next time you participate in an activity with someone, ask that person: "What do you think is going on?" "Why is this happening?" Then compare the response to your own.*

Our ability to be self-reflective and to think, feel, and act in our own manner is fundamental to most counseling and some therapies. In such therapeutic situations the goal is to alter one's self and one's life. Success, however, depends upon each client's capacity to project new ways of living and to become engaged in them. Many succeed. People in all stages of life make changes in themselves. Some draw upon the expertise of professionals; others do not. Learning to do things differently is actually quite commonplace.

Once we recognize our capacity for independent thought, feeling and action, we can decide how we will tap into it. We can choose to continue living as we always have. Or we can set about doing things in a new way: We can reflect on what we would like to do; explore our environment for a means of doing it; determine the steps to be taken; and proceed to follow them.

If you believe that you can be aware of yourself, that you can generate your own ideas, and that you can map out new courses of action for yourself, then please consider the following questions:

- *Do I want to change myself and the way I live?*
- *Do I want to do whatever it takes to make this happen, or do I want to leave things just as they are?*

Each of us will respond in our own unique way. Our reactions will be governed by who we are and how we view our selves and our lives. Each response will be conditioned by the degree to which we accept the status quo; by our desire for changing our selves and the way we live; by our drive to pursue these goals; and by our persistence in working for them.

You may see no good reason for altering the way you live. Perhaps everything is fine just as it is. And so you have no desire to change a thing.

Or you may think: Yes, there are very good reasons for living differently. But perhaps you don't want to bother doing anything—it's too much of a hassle, too complicated, and just not worth it.

On the other hand, you may want to try living in another way. And making the necessary changes seems like a worthwhile challenge.

- *Choices: Pursue a new goal? Leave things just as they are? Once again, it's up to you.*

Let's now turn to questions that many have asked throughout the ages: Is developing the moral dimension of our selves and our lives an option for us? Do we have inborn traits of "self-centeredness" and aggressiveness that render ethical living unattainable?

The answer to the first question is yes! And the reply to the second one is no! In short, we *can* choose to become more ethical. Of course, in a competitive world this may not be immediately apparent. For there we often meet more self-centered persons than empathetic-giving ones and more people who devalue each other than lend support. Nevertheless, the prevalence of one way of relating does not prove that the other is unnatural or impossible.

Moral living is a viable option for us. Indeed, we find one of its building blocks, empathy, appearing early in life. Infants cry in response to another's crying. Older children express unhappiness when someone is upset and frequently offer solace by hugging the person in distress.

Empathy may continue to develop, or it may not. The environment in which we live can nurture or diminish it.[39]

Our surroundings do, in fact, influence us. But, don't forget, we affect them as well! By repeatedly interacting with self-serving and aggressive people, we're apt to expect such behavior from everyone. Then we may even act as if this were the case all the time. When we function this way, we engage in a self-fulfilling prophecy. By constantly defending our behavior, undermining others, and making excuses for doing so—*we ourselves* reinforce and perpetuate this mode of living.

To better understand the moral dimension in your own life, ask yourself:

- *Have I felt more concern for others and been more eager to extend myself to them at certain times rather than others?*
- *When did I want to reach out to them, and when did I not want to?*
- *What were the situations like?*
- *Why did I feel that way?*
- *Do I take advantage of others whenever I have a chance?*
- *Do I act this way only on occasion? If so, when? Why?*

Every kind of personal change has its own requirements. In the next section we'll explore one avenue for self-development—moral growth.

As you continue to read, if you're open to modifying the way you live, ask: Do I want to make the effort to become more ethical? Is it worthwhile?

Ethical Change

In one respect, integrating a moral orientation into our lives is similar to making other changes within our selves. It's like modifying our eating patterns, starting to exercise, or altering our responses to others. In each instance, change occurs when our thoughts, perceptions or actions have been replaced with new ones.[40]

But unlike many skills and habits, ethical actions *always* involve other people and usually occur while we are interacting directly with them. That is to say, our actions are considered moral because of the way we intend to act toward others, the way we do in fact act toward them, and the effects our actions have on them.

Over time the people with whom we live will become aware of the ethical or unethical character of our actions. Their responses to our deeds can run the gamut from gratitude and appreciation to negative criticism and outright ostracism. These reactions impact on us. They can either encourage us to continue being ethical or they can be discouraging negative forces.

The people in our midst profoundly affect our ethical development. So it is imperative to consider who they are. The significance of others in moral development renders this kind of personal change more complicated than others.

Once we've chosen to live ethically, we may ask ourselves: How can I become more consistently moral?

Let's turn to this question now.

Chapter XII

ഇൗൽ

How to Dig Out

Myself and Others

To set the stage for our next discussion, let's remind ourselves that many of the things we do—such as putting lemon in our tea, wearing our hair short, riding a bicycle to school, and eating six times a day—primarily involve ourselves. Acting morally is not one of them. Since ethical actions take place in relation to others, the people with whom we interact affect our moral life.

When we're ethical, those who do not appreciate our way of living are likely to think we're jerks. They do not realize that kindness stems from strength. To them compassion is just a sign of weakness. They might even try to use our feelings of concern to their own advantage.

Very simply, living ethically among immoral people is difficult, frequently unpleasant, and potentially harmful.

If we want to live morally, we should strive to be with people who appreciate the kind of person we are and respond to us accordingly.

Whenever we trust moral people, they treat us with care. They give us no reason to be defensive. Talking with them about our way of life strengthens our capacity to trust. We get along as a team with the same goal—the best life for each of us. Associating with them validates, supports, and reinforces us and our common approach to living.

But, of course, not everyone functions in this manner; we can only expect some individuals to be kind and considerate.

Who are they?

How can we find them?

Well, for a start, we can discover the trustworthy ones by observing what people do. This means taking a chance. For we do need to trust people to ascertain how they will treat us. One way of testing the waters is to depend on someone when the issues at stake are not very important. What's the response? Does he or she still seem worthy of our confidence? If so, we have the go-ahead to place our faith in this person again.

As we continue to trust others, we will gain a better understanding of them; and we will develop appropriate ways of interacting. By repeatedly relying on people, we can more readily recognize who is actually worthy of our confidence. Then we can more assuredly select such persons as associates, companions, and friends.

But wait a minute—let me ask you: Do you really want to live among trustworthy people?

This may sound like a foolish question, but it's not. Living among such people may be new for you. If it is, you may need to change.

Making this change is similar to modifying other aspects of how we live. From the beginning, we have to be sure we want it. And once the decision has been made, we need to chose our actions thoughtfully. Determination, care, and vigilance are required.

Let's remember: change always involves embarking on the unknown.[41] This can be scary! Moreover, unsettling feelings of awkwardness and discomfort are often stirred up. Modifying our approach life is much harder than most other kinds of change, such as getting a new job or moving to a different town. As internal change takes place, old habits of thinking, feeling and doing are replaced by new ones. With persistent effort and courage we can give up the comfortable for the unknown.

So it is not at all suprising that most personal change occurs very slowly. Moreover, some people succeed briefly—only to revert to a former state, while others seem unable to alter their own thoughts, feelings, and actions in any way whatsoever.

If this sounds dreadful, you may be asking yourself: Why should I try to change?

My answer is simply this: You and I are already creating our selves as we live. So why not mold your self into someone you'd like to live with?[42]

I'm surely not the only one to have ever thought this way. Many people today, as well as throughout history, have firmly believed that we can learn better ways to conduct ourselves. Some have even viewed self-change as a major goal.

- *Have you ever tried to modify one of your habits?*
- *Or have you known people who have attempted to alter how they live?*
- *What were the results?*

Saying "It's good to change" is easy. Making it happen is always more difficult.

What might we *do* to facilitate our own moral growth?

For starters, we can reflect on the actions of people who live ethically. We may find these individuals almost anywhere—for example, among our daily acquaintances; in newspapers, television and movies; and through novels and historical accounts. As models of ethical living, they show us who we can be. And they demonstrate why it's good to live morally.

We also would do well to stay away from those who make light of our efforts and deny their validity, or who are careless with us. For being with them is tantamount to placing obstacles in our way.

On the other hand, discussing our goals with supportive people can make it easier to remain on our chosen path. By just listening to those who believe in our way of life, we can become more certain of what we're about. And the positive energy such people emanate is encouraging in itself.[43]

Informal conversations with like-minded friends can reinforce our ethical way of life. So can attending more formalized support networks that meet with some regularity.

Structured self-help groups—such as Overeaters Anonymous, various men's and women's groups, Debtors Anonymous, AA, and Al-Anon—have had a good track record in facilitating a wide array of personal changes. So there is every reason to believe that discussions concerning the development of moral life can also be useful. To test this out, talk with ethical people about your own moral concerns.

Environments

The point just made here is a simple one, based on common sense. It is this: the easiest way to live as we want is to stay away from obstacles and to surround ourselves with support.

We've already seen that we can facilitate moral living by choosing to live with ethical people. Another way is by selecting and shaping our environments.

- *Ask yourself: Do the situations I find myself in affirm me as a moral person?*
- *At work: Is business conducted so that no harm is done to employees, business associates or others? Are my tasks detrimental to myself or others? How do my work associates treat one another? Is the tone of the workplace conducive to self-respect and consideration for others? Is the goal of the enterprise a moral one?*
- *At school: What are the most prevalent attitudes and feelings? How do the teachers conduct their classes? How do they relate to their students? How do the students interact with one another and with their instructors?*
- *With friends: How do my friends treat me? Do I feel comfortable and good about myself when I'm with them? Do I feel like giving to them?*
- *In recreation: What feelings does the activity itself stir up within me? How am I expected to act while participating? When I am playing a game, does team spirit or fierce competition set the tone? Is the locale friendly?*

Now, if you believe that a setting in which you've spent time has not been supportive of moral living, you can ask yourself:

- *Can I change the way things are done?*
- *Can I improve my role?*

If you find that the organization, institution, business, or group with which you are associated is harmful to you and that, as a participant, you have no way of preventing this—there is still something you can do.

You can begin by asking yourself:

- *Should I end my affiliation? Leave the job? Stop playing the game? Keep my distance from that place? Avoid spending time with those people?*
- *Or should I go to an outside authority—a person or group— that can change the way things are done? Should I "blow the whistle"?*

Once acting morally is integrated into our selves, we will be more capable of sustaining an ethical way of life when there's little or no external support. In time, we may be able to infuse a moral point of view into situations which do not affirm ethical living. But, as always, how we exercise our abilities is up to us.[44]

Having had this discussion, let's return to society at large and look at the deterrents to ethical living lodged within it. This time around, however, I'd like to focus on how we might keep these elements from eroding our moral lives.

Violence Is Not Good for Your Health

Now, why is "violence" our topic?

I bet you know. It's because the aggressive attitudes and approaches to life found among the violent hinder ethical living. These mind-sets and behaviors are likely to be present even when physical violence is not. For as we've already noted, these attitudes—under the guise of competitiveness—pervade modern society.

What can we do to counteract these deterrents to moral life?

At the start, we can *reject* the cliches that support competitiveness: "Look out for #1" and "It's either him or me."

To *neutralize* these win-lose attitudes for ourselves, we can first remember that they're not true and then focus on what is.

"Either/or" thinking often does not apply to moral situations. As we've already discussed: When people are generous, everyone involved benefits; and when "looking out for #1" is my way of life, I harm myself. If we keep these ideas in mind, we can more readily avoid falling prey to destructive thoughts.

But eliminating erroneous beliefs is not enough. We also need an effective means of functioning with the competitive, violent and unethical behaviors prevalent in contemporary society. Studies have shown that being in the presence of such behavior—even if it is not directed toward us—erodes the very foundation of our moral life, trust in others.[45]

Of course, there is no easy way to completely eliminate destructive behavior from society at large. But we can usually exercise some control over our own exposure to real and vicarious experiences of it.

Success in this task requires a conscious effort. We need to step outside the regular flow of living to understand and assess the *people* with whom we associate, as well as *what* we do, and *where* and *how* we do it. With this information in mind, we can better determine what is best for us.

When we choose to live morally among those who are not ethical, some people and situations may change through our example. Others do not. On occasion, making the reasons for our moral behavior known can generate understanding and may even influence some to consider changing their ways. Yet, at other times, this information will be used against us.

What to do? There are no rules here. Only our judgment can preside.

- *What are the deterrents to ethical living in your life? How do you want to handle them?*

Running Away

To be sure, external sources are not the only deterrents to moral living. We can create our own roadblocks.

Let's take a look at a few.

For one, there is escapism. We can keep ourselves from becoming moral by detaching from what's real. It is easy to assume this mode, for there are many people around to copy.

Here are a few examples of roads they may take.

Addiction is among the most frequently taken avoidance routes. Substance abuse is just one of them. It's common knowledge that addicts focus exclusively on securing their drug of choice. Taking it distorts their perception of reality. And the users are left with impaired knowledge.

As a consequence, their capacity to appreciate their own selves, their surroundings and their lives is severely weakened. What's more, their reasoning ability is damaged. Thus, for them living morally is rendered impossible.

Another way of "running away" is to keep ourselves busy always doing something or another. Busyness can take many forms: We can, for instance, listen to music or watch television at every spare moment; or we can bury ourselves in work, never allowing ourselves an opportunity to take in new experiences or to think about anything.

Negative deterministic thinking is another escape route. Such a mind-set permits us to retreat from engaging in life. For this point of view assumes that nothing is worth doing and nothing can be changed. Pessimism can be found in all sorts of people—among our friends, co-workers, acquaintances, members of our family. . . . When we embrace this attitude, we feel justified in doing nothing. For we're convinced there's no reason to do anything. This kind of negative thinking and its concomitant inaction preclude moral choice.

Now, of course, not all avenues for escape are bad in themselves. Retreating from life's responsibilities is not necessarily destructive to us, nor is it always a deterrent to moral living. There's certainly nothing wrong with securing some relief from all the demands placed on us. Having fun is terrific! And through our work we can become more fully engaged in living.

How avoidance routes affect us is very much in our own hands. For their impact on us is determined by how *we* integrate them into our lives. Let's remember that when escapism dominates our lives, we're no longer able to appreciate ourselves or others. And we live accordingly.

- *Do you have ways to escape?*
- *What effects do they have on you?*
- *Are they worth doing?*
- *If your answer is "Yes, they are worth doing," ask yourself: Why?*
- *If you think you should do things differently, ask yourself: How else can I live?*

Making It Happen

Creating an ethical life requires awareness, reflection and time. It is an *ongoing process*.

Fostering an ethical life is a way of shaping our selves and our lives. As we've already observed in our section on violence, to gain some control over our lives, we need to *take a break* from doing and producing. Without this pause we're likely to do things the way we've always done them. Or we're apt to be heavily influenced by the modes of thinking, feeling and acting around us. When we're freed up for thinking, we can distance ourselves from whatever is going on and avoid succumbing to our immediate responses.

The current situation may then be examined and assessed. Through *reflection*, we may notice ways of coping with it. Next, after evaluating our capacity to realize the available options, we can begin to *discern* the best course of action. And, once the path is determined, we need to *act*.

Discovering how an environment can be supportive of moral living takes time and effort. Shaping one requires even more. Always rushing about, making snap judgments, and complying with every demand upon request are inevitably counterproductive to us. To make the best decisions possible, we need a pace and a frame of mind that keep us grounded in reality.

~ ~ ~ ~ ~ ~ ~ ~ ~ ~ ~ ~ ~ ~ ~ ~ ~ ~ ~ ~

Remarks

ಬಾ

I've known many people who have lived morally, embracing life and caring about others. But before we close, I'd like to tell you about three who made a lasting impression on me..

My high school math teacher, Miss McGrevy, was unlike many other instructors I had. When I studied with her, she had already taught for many years but was not "burned out." It was obvious that Miss McGrevy cared very much about her students and still gleaned satisfaction from her work. She was a person of few words, but most of us knew how she felt. We could sense her acute sensitivity and devotion in everything she did.

My friend Jack was also in her class. He was an excellent student who enjoyed school. However, severe financial pressures and a negative self-image prevented him from considering a college education. When Miss McGrevy heard this, she was stunned and outraged.

As planned, soon after commencement ceremonies Jack went to work for a wholesale distributor. But he could not forget Miss McGrevy's reactions. Later on he decided to attend college part-time. As he wrestled with his financial problems and self-doubts, Miss McGrevy's belief in him repeatedly came to mind. It sustained him in college, right through graduation.

There's also my former student Patrice, who like many in my classes had the pressures of a full-time college program and a job. Nevertheless, she went to a child-welfare agency seeking someone to befriend. There she met Melissa, a parentless young girl. Patrice deftly juggled the existing demands in her life to make room for regular visits with Melissa. Both looked forward to their times together. The "big-sister" relationship and friendship that developed between them seemed mutually rewarding.

And then there's my Uncle Frank, whom I knew very well. He was a person who worked hard to provide a modest life for his wife and young child. When the workday was over, he devoted his attention to the family, made necessary repairs on their small house, and participated in local community projects.

In spite of my uncle's many commitments, when his brother Ben had neither a job nor a place to live, Frank rallied to his side. My Uncle Frank converted the attic in his house into living space, invited Ben into his home, and helped him get re-established.

Another time my Uncle Frank took two of his friends aside to tell them he thought they could treat their little boy Robert with more care. And he hoped they would stop venting their frustrations on the child. However, the couple rejected Frank's suggestions. So after that, my uncle made it a point to treat Robert as a very special person. He wanted the boy to know that someone was on his side.

My Uncle Frank enjoyed taking people on picnics. After going fishing, he would invariably give some of his catch to others.

Frank loved life and people. And people liked him. So no one was surprised when he quickly secured customers for his home-heating-oil business.

- *Do you know someone like Miss McGrevy, Patrice or Frank?*
- *How did he or she affect you?*

~ ~

Yes, we have come to the end of our discussion. Let's wrap it up by reminding ourselves of a few key points:

How we live shapes us and our world.

An ethical life occurs only when we choose it.

Living morally is worthwhile.

Moreover, it is easier to live ethically when we (1) avoid the push to be competitive, (2) decrease our exposure to all forms of violence, and (3) stay in touch with life.

But we'll live morally within an ethical community *only* if we *want* it enough to make it happen.

NOTES

INTRODUCTION

1 In using "moral" and "immoral" interchangeably with "ethical" and "unethical," respectively, I am adopting a common practice. Kai Nielsen (1967), "Ethics," in Paul Edwards (Ed. in chief), *Encyclo-pedia of Philosophy*, Vol. 3 (New York: Free Press) makes no distinction between these two words. You might want to read his discussion and those entitled "Ethical Relativism," "Ethical Subjectivism," "Ethics, History of," and "Ethics, Problems of."

CHAPTER II

2 Socrates, an ancient Greek philosopher, lived by ethical values. His interactions with people in ancient Athens who were not living with ethical values are portrayed in Plato's early dialogues, e.g., the "Apology." See Edith Hamilton and Huntington Cairns (Eds.) (1984), *Collected Dialogues of Plato* (Princeton: Princeton University Press).

3 Many philosophers have written about people who treat others as if they were objects. This is a recurring theme for Existentialists. The play "No Exit" by Jean-Paul Sartre (1955), *No Exit and Three Other Plays* (New York: Random House), vividly depicts such interpersonal relationships.

4 People who think in this way designate certain types of acts "good" and others "bad." This means that a wrong kind of act (e.g., lying, stealing, cheating, etc.) is always wrong. The conditions under which it occurs—where, when or toward whom—can never change a "wrong act" into a "right act." The form of an act

makes it wrong. Immanuel Kant typifies this formalist approach to ethics. Introductory ethics texts and encyclopedias of philosophy are good places to read more about formalism. See Lawrence C. Becker (Ed.) and Charlotte B. Becker (Associate Ed.) (1992), *Encyclopedia of Ethics* (New York: Garland Publishing, Inc.).

5   Utilitarians (such as Jeremy Bentham and John Stuart Mill) and American pragmatists (such as John Dewey) approach ethics in this way. Introductory ethics texts and encyclopedias of philosophy will tell you more about this philosophical orientation. See also Jeremy Bentham (1988), *Principles of Morals and Legislation* (Amherst, NY: Prometheus Books) and John Stuart Mill (1993), Geraint Williams (Ed.), *Utilitarianism, On Liberty, Considerations on Representative Government* (Boston: C. E. Tuttle); John Dewey (1960) provides a brief description of instrumentalism in *The Quest for Certainty* (New York: Capricorn Books), chap. X, and a more extensive account of it in Dewey (1922), JoAnne Boydston (Ed.), *Human Nature and Conduct* (Illinois: South Illinois University Press).

6   By seeking a family of characteristics, my approach in this book draws from an idea the philosopher Ludwig Wittgenstein developed in his later works. See: Ludwig Wittgenstein (1973), *Philosophical Investigations* (New York: Macmillan), I sec. 7, 23, 66-67, 69 and 79; Ludwig Wittgenstein (1942), *Brown Book* (New York: Harper Collins), II sec. 2, 3, and 14. Wittgenstein wrote that we get a sense of the meaning of a word by observing its use and by using it. You can get an appreciation of his point by trying to define the word "game." Think about the ways in which games are alike and the way they differ from each other. Do you know something is a game because you know a list of characteristics for all games? How do you know something is a game?

CHAPTER III

7   If you are interested in reading about the role of caring in moral life, I suggest that you read Nell Noddings (1984), *Caring* (Berkeley, CA: University of California Press) and others who have a feminist approach to ethics. See note #9.

8   David Hume (1991), an 18th-century Scottish philosopher, developed the idea that morality is based on feelings that are natural to us in *A Treatise of Human Nature* (New York: Prometheus Books). See Bk. 2, pt. 3, sec. 3 and Bk. 3, pt. 3, sec. 6.

9   See Carol Gilligan, "Moral Orientation and Moral Development," in Eva Feder Kittay and Diana T. Meyers (Eds.) (1987), *Women and Moral Theory* (Totowa, NJ: Rowman & Littlefield), pp. 19-33.

10 Plato perceived the aesthetic dimension of life and love as interrelated with the good.

Iris Murdoch (1971), a British fiction writer and philosopher, in *The Sovereignty of Good* (New York: Schocken Books, Inc.), develops the idea that reality needs to be penetrated if we are to be moral.

Mary Midgley (1981), *Heart and Mind* (New York: St. Martin's Press), chap. 1, explores the role of feelings in a moral life.

11 The psychologist and educator Harvey A. Hornstein (1976) wrote extensively about the development of the feeling "we" in his book *Cruelty and Kindness* (New Jersey: Prentice-Hall). Many examples and studies are included. Martin L. Hoffman (1984), "Empathy, Social Cognition and Moral Action," in W. Kurtines and J. Gerwitz (Eds.), *Moral Behavior and Development* (New York: John Wiley and Sons), makes the case that the roots of morality lie in empathy.

12 The ancient Greek philosopher Aristotle maintained that our character develops through our actions. See Aristotle (1980), W. David Ross trans., *Nichomachean Ethics* (New York: Oxford University Press).

The ideas that as we live in different ways, we create different selves, and that some selves are sympathetic and expansive, while others are not—were espoused by William James (1985), an American pragmatic philosopher/psychologist, Gordon Allport (Ed.), *Psychology (A Briefer Course)* (Notre Dame, IND: University of Notre Dame Press), chap. 12, "Self."

John Dewey, another American pragmatic philosopher, describes us as always interacting with our surroundings, whereby mutual modification is always occurring. These ideas are made explicit in John Dewey (1929), *Experience and Nature* (Mineola, NY: Dover).

Anthropologists have described cultures in which people learn aggression and others in which they learn nonviolence. See, for example, Ashley Montagu (Ed.) (1978), *Learning Non-Aggression* (New York: Oxford University Press).

CHAPTER IV

13 John Stuart Mill, a 19th-century English philosopher, discusses these values in *On Liberty*. See note #5.
14 In *Freedom and Culture* (Illinois: Waveland Press), the anthropologist Dorothy Lee (1987) describes ways in which a family's cultural context influences its values. The values, in turn, affect their actions, including their treatment of children. In response to this environment, children develop values and ways of behaving. William James (1990), "Pragmatism and Common Sense," *Pragmatism* (New York: Prometheus Books), offers an explanation for the way in which ideas are changed, preserved in common sense, and learned by children. Several theories of moral development can be found in Paul Crittenden (1990), *Learning to be Moral* (New Jersey: Humanities Press International, Inc.). William Damon (1988), *The Moral Child* (New York: Free Press), presents an exemplary integration of current thinking on morality of young children. See also note #5: John Dewey, *Human Nature and Conduct*, pt. I, sec. 1.
15 William James and John Dewey write about habits of mind. Dewey maintains that the major task of education is teaching people how to think. See note #5.
16 A wide array of moral dilemmas occuring in the delivery of health care services can be found in numerous bioethics and medical ethics anthologies, as well as in the *Hastings Center Report* (1978) (Briarcliff Manor, NY: Hastings Center). Some works focus narrowly on the ethical problems that may arise within one area of health and medicine, e.g., Helen B. Holmes (1992), *Issues in Reproductive Technology I* (New York: Garland).

CHAPTER V

17 Many Existentialist philosophers are concerned about people who live as if they were inert objects. Jean-Paul Sartre (1975) has

written extensively about this. In the essay "Existentialism is a Humanism," he describes some risks and responsibilities involved in making our own decisions. This essay can be found in many anthologies, e.g., Walter Kaufman (Ed.)(1975), *Existentialism from Dostoyevsky to Sartre* (New York: Dutton). To read further about the creation of meaning, you can start with Jerome S. Bruner (1990), *Acts of Meaning* (Cambridge, MA: Harvard University Press) and Mark Johnson (1987), *The Body in the Mind* (Illinois: University of Chicago Press).

18 Martin Buber (1958) in *I and Thou* (New York: Charles Scribner's Sons) develops the idea of people who are detached from themselves and others, living in I-It relationships. This idea is further explicated in essay form in Martin Buber (1965), *Between Man and Man* (New York: Macmillan Publishing Co., Inc.), I section 1 "Observing, Looking On, Becoming Aware," "The Signs," and "Responsibility."

CHAPTER VI

19 Existentialist philosophers are concerned with the significance of the act of taking responsibility for ourselves; see *Existentialism from Dostoyevsky to Sartre*, note #17. Jean-Paul Sartre depicts people who have not taken responsibility for their own lives and blame others for who they are in "No Exit"; see note #3.

CHAPTER VII

20 John Dewey maintains that people develop themselves by how they live. At each point in time who we have become sets the framework for engaging in our experiences. Dewey (1963) explored the implications of these ideas in many of his works and developed their significance for education in *Experience and Education* (New York: Macmillan), chap. 3; and in Dewey (1966), *Democracy and Education* (New York: Macmillan), chap. 4.

21 Friedrich Nietzsche (1978), a 19th-century philosopher, found himself in a world that had no meanings or values of its own. Meanings and values exist, he maintained, only when we experience them as real; and without our creativity there would be none. He wrote of the process of making meanings and the

need to do so in *Thus Spoke Zarasthustra*, Walter Kaufmann trans. (New York: Viking). Anthony Earl of Shaftesbury (1900) provides an extended discusion of enthusiasm in *Characteristics of Men, Manners, Opinions, Times, etc.*, Vol.I, treatise 1 (London: Grant Richards).

22 Many who approach health holistically have recognized the relationship between the level of stress, the onset of illness, and the absence of supportive people in a person's life. See, for example, the writings of Leonard J. Duhl.

23 It is very difficult to describe happiness. An early attempt to develop an understanding of it was made by Aristotle in the *Nicomachean Ethics*, chap. 1, 7, and 12; see note #12.

CHAPTER VIII

24 For a readily accessible discussion of these conflicting positions, ethical relativism and ethical absolutism, see K. Richard Garrett (1990), *Dialogues Concerning the Foundations of Ethics* (Maryland: Rowman & Littlefield Publishers, Inc.).

25 When a pragmatic approach is taken, the meaning and the significance of an action, for example, is determined by how it functions and the effects it produces. This way of seeking truth was articulated by the American Pragmatists (Charles Saunders Peirce, William James and John Dewey) in the late 19th and early 20th centuries. William James wrote about the pragmatic approach in *Pragmatism* (note #14); and he applied it to the study of religion in William James (1958), *The Varieties of Religious Experience* (New York: Penguin).

26 Seyla Benhabib (1992), in *Situating the Self* (New York: Routledge), discusses the relationship between social bonds and moral obligation.

27 See note #22 and note #12 for Aristotle VIII 3 and IX 4-9.

28 Lord Shaftesbury (note #21) maintained that as we act morally and recognize people's worth and merit, we experience happiness, since this behavior is compatible with our natural social nature; also see note #11.

29 The cognitive psychologist Albert Ellis wrote that having rational control over our life can positively effect our general well-being. Consequently, therapy should center on developing rational control

of our own life. See, for example, Albert Ellis (1988), *Rational Emotive Therapy* (Needham Heights, MA: Allyn). Holistic health practitioners have written on the relationship between feeling we have control over our lives and experiencing stress. See also note #23.

30 The physician Herbert Benson (1992) describes the human body's response to relaxation in *The Relaxation Response* (New York: Random), a book readily accessible to the general reader.

31 Norman Cousins (1983) relates his experiences combatting ankylosing spondylitis with laughter in *Anatomy of an Illness as Perceived by the Patient* (New York: Bantam).

32 See note #22.

33 An extensive treatment of the nature of lying can be found in Sissela Bok (1978), *Lying* (New York: Pantheon Books).

CHAPTER IX

34 *The New American Bible*, trans. by members of the Catholic Biblical Association of America (1970) (New York: Collier-Macmillan Limited).

35 *Ibid.*

36 There are many reflections on the relationship between moral people and their society in Aristotle's *Nichomachean Ethics* (note #12) and in Plato's dialogues (note #2); the "Republic," a Platonic dialogue, develops a theory regarding people's roles within an ideal society.

CHAPTER X

37 See note #18 Buber (1965), p. 103.

38 *Ibid.*, p. 104.

CHAPTER XI

39 David Hume (note #8). A science journalist, Matt Ridley (1997), *The Origins of Virtue* (New York: Viking), presents an excellent guide to competing theories in the debate on the natural foundation

for morality. Frans de Waal (1996), *Good Natured* (Cambridge, MA: Harvard University Press), p. 5, makes the case that the foundation for human morality is in nature. J. Philippe Rushton & Richard M. Sorrentino (Eds.), *Altruism and Helping Behavior* (Hillsdale, NJ: Lawrence Enlbaum) offer a comprehensive account of altruism from a psychological point of view. Alfie Kohn (1990), *The Brighter Side of Human Nature* (New York: Harper Collins), discusses the prevalence of altrusim and empathy in everyday life. See also notes #11 and #27.

40 John Dewey (note #12).

CHAPTER XII

41 Existential philosophers have written about the anxiety and dread experienced while making decisions. There are numerous collections of existentialists' ideas; for example, see note #17 and Wade Baskin (Ed.) (1993), *Essays in Existentialism* (New York: Citadel).

42 The idea of creating our selves as we live has been explored by many people; among whom we find Aristotle, John Dewey, and Jean-Paul Sartre; see notes #12, #20 and #39.

43 The positive energy emitted from people in a social setting is on a continuum with the energy that provides therapeutic touch with power for healing. This alternative form of treatment has been accepted in some settings where traditional medicine is practiced.

44 Existential philosophers, psychologists and theologians (e.g., Jean-Paul Sartre, Erich Fromm and Paul Tillich) have explored the isolation experienced when making choices. See note #39.

45 See note #11.